VirtualMedia

A Step-By-Step Techniques Guide

Edited By
Kathleen Ziegler and Nick Greco

Watson-Guptill

HBI
Hearst Books International

First Published 1999 by
Dimensional Illustrators, Inc.
For Hearst Books International
1350 Avenue of the Americas
New York, NY 10019
ISBN: 1-885660-16-2

Distributed in the U.S. and Canada by
Watson-Guptill Publications
1515 Broadway
New York, NY 10036
800-451-1741 Phone
732-363-4511 in NJ, AK, HI
732-363-0338 Fax
ISBN: 0-8230-6983-4

Distributed throughout the rest of the world by
Hearst Books International
1350 Avenue of the Americas
New York, NY 10019 USA
212-261-6795 Fax

First Published in Germany by
NIPPAN
Nippon Shuppan Hanbai
Deutschland GmbH
Krefelder Str. 85
D-40549 Dusseldorf
0211-5048089 Telephone
0211-5049326 Fax
ISBN: 3-931884-50-3

©Copyright 1999 by Dimensional Illustrators, Inc.
and Hearst Books International

Address Direct Mail Sales to
Dimensional Illustrators, Inc.
362 Second Street Pike / Suite 112
Southampton, PA 18966 USA
Email: dimension@3dimillus.com
Website: http://www.3dimillus.com
215-953-1415 Phone
215-953-1697 Fax

Printed in Hong Kong

VirtualMedia Credits

CREATIVE DIRECTOR/ASSOCIATE EDITOR
Kathleen Ziegler / Dimensional Illustrators, Inc.

EXECUTIVE EDITOR
Nick Greco / Dimensional Illustrators, Inc.

BOOK DESIGN, JACKET COVER DESIGN & TYPOGRAPHY
Deborah Davis / Deborah Davis Design

COPYWRITER
Cathy Fishel/Catharine & Sons

COVER ART
FRONT COVER - Tony Klassen
FRONT COVER INSET ART - Susan LeVan, Jason Howard Statts, Tom White
BACK COVER INSET ART - Yasutaka Taga, Jenson Designaholix, Margaret Carsello, Scott Petty
CONTENTS PAGE INSET ART - Lisa Johnston, Tony Klassen, Chet Phillips, Gustavo Machado, Rafael Peixoto Ferreira

Table of Contents

INTRODUCTION

As an art tool, the computer has carved a path that allows artists to express themselves with unlimited spontaneity. The new digital canvas has fused fresh methods and traditional techniques into a fresh, exciting medium. In this one-of-a-kind collection, digital aficionados reveal their approaches through twelve step-by-step projects that demonstrate their creative acumen. The five chapters Digital Collage, 3D Modeling, CyberIllustration, Filters and Effects, and

Typography—share a cross-section of a unique range of techniques. Each artist draws us into his or her cyber-world of artistic interpretation through a variety of software, including Adobe Photoshop, MetaCreations Fractal Painter, Adobe Dimensions, Expression Tools' Shade, Pixar Typestry, RayDream Designer, Adobe Illustrator, and Cheap Video Trick. Virtual tips from each artist offer software shortcuts and insights for the virtual designer. Drop-down menu commands are highlighted to make understanding the programs easy. As each step-by-step project unfolds, follow along as the final image develops on the page. Then use the book's directory of website addresses to download demonstration software featured in this book. You'll learn how layers, light, shadows, blurring, textures, color washes, photographs and simple lines can merge in a masterful blend of pixels.

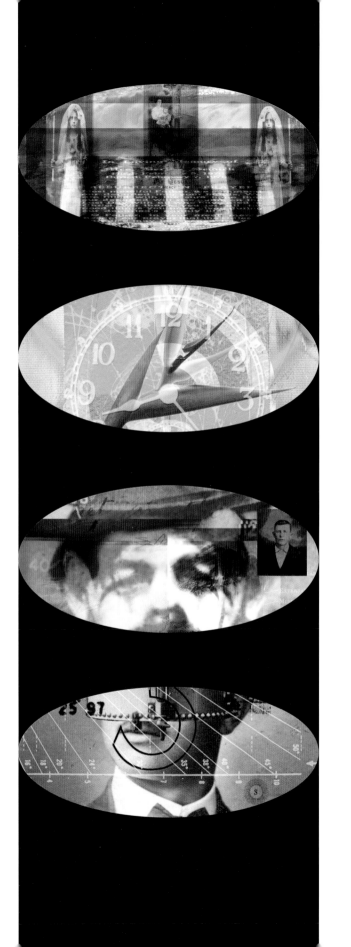

DIGITAL
COLLAGE

The real and the remembered are woven together in digital

collage. Using Adobe Photoshop, the artists featured in this

section all use intricate, minute layering in their art but

inject their own personal flair as well. Lisa Johnston

combines her photography with a host of symbolic icons,

while Margaret Carsello creates with color, painting and

photographs. Jason Statts is inspired by the visual debris

of found objects, and Scott Petty brings together real and

imagined ghosts from his past. All tell stories that touch

on our own personal and visceral experiences.

Holy See

PURPOSE sacred places series
DIGITAL CREATIVE lisa johnston
SOFTWARE adobe photoshop

Lisa
JOHnSTON

Lisa Johnston feels that the computer is only an

implement of our contemporary culture—simply an

icon in the futuristic banquet of aesthetics available

today. But she uses it as a vehicle to conduct a

physical and spiritual search of holy grounds. For

instance, her "Sacred Places" series was inspired by

a personal quest to relate her own religious beliefs to

the beliefs of others. The artist uses Adobe Photoshop

to intertwine religious symbols and photos of sacred

creating the background layer

A. A photograph of an ocean scene was scanned into Adobe Photoshop.

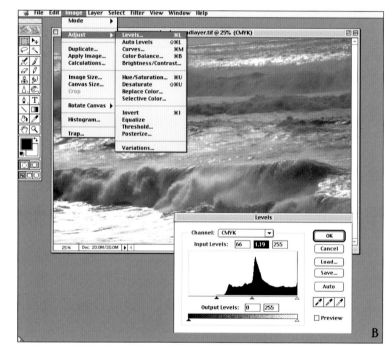

B. The color was adjusted by selecting **Image›Adjust›Levels**. In the Levels dialog box, the level sliders were moved in the shadow and highlight areas to balance the brightness, contrast and midtones of the image.

C. The ocean scene was saved as the Background Layer by choosing **Window›Show Layers**. This was the base image of the montage. Other layers were added as the piece progressed.

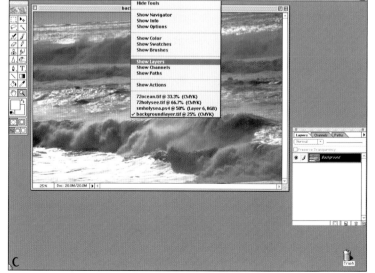

VirtualMedia A Step-By-Step Techniques Guide

final image

creating layer 1

1A

1A. The first layer was composed from a stock image of ancient columns opened in Adobe Photoshop.

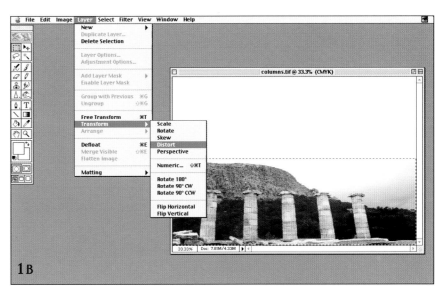

1B

1B. The entire image was selected with the Marquee Tool. Then using **Layer › Transform › Distort**, the columns were compressed to fit the bottom third of the canvas area. The entire image area was then selected with the Marquee Tool and [⌘Command Key+C] was used to copy the area.

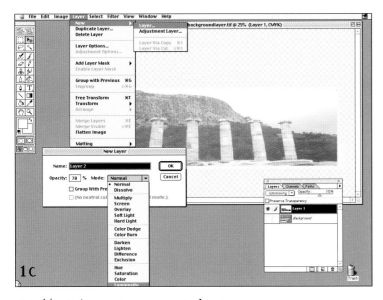

1C

1C. Next, Layer 1 was created using **Layer › New › Layer**. As the dialog box with Layer 1 opened, Opacity: 70% and Mode: Luminosity were selected.

1D. The layer was finalized by making the Layer 1 window active with the Move Tool and using [⌘Command Key+V] to paste the image into the layer. **Layer › Layer Options** was chosen and the information about the layer was confirmed.

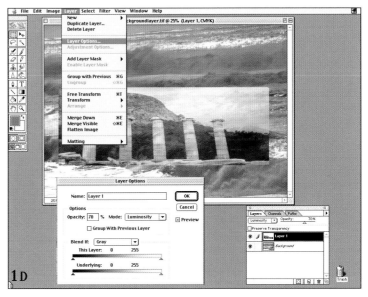

1D

creating layer 2

2A. A photograph of Pope John Paul II was scanned into Adobe Photoshop. Several images were made from this photo to create the montage for Layer 2.

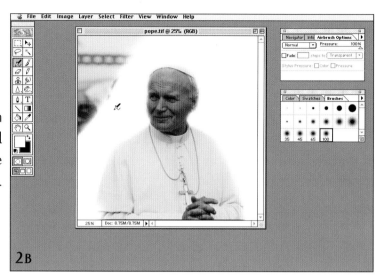

2B. Using the Airbrush Tool, the background was removed by airbrushing white around the perimeter of the figure.

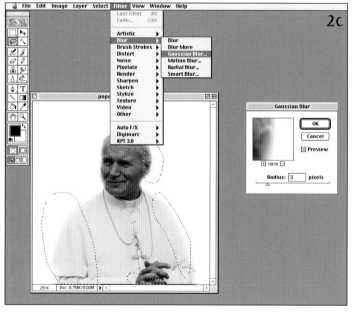

2C. Using the Lasso Tool, areas of the figure were selected. Using **Filter › Blur › Gaussian Blur**, a lightly blurred effect was implemented. A radius of 3 pixels achieved this effect.

2D. Since the balance of the Pope's flesh tone was too saturated, the adjustment sliders under **Image › Adjust › Levels** were used to desaturate the magenta.

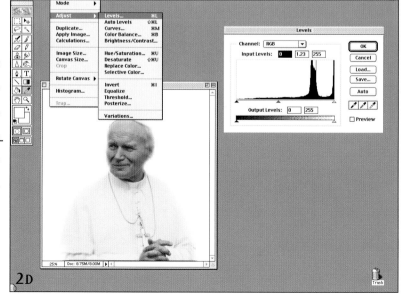

VirtualMedia A Step-By-Step Techniques Guide

final image

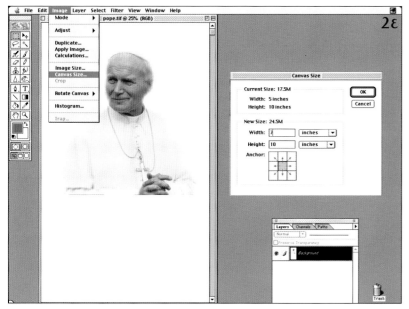

2ε. To prepare the initial piece for the montage, the canvas size of the Pope's image was first enlarged with **Image›Canvas Size** , and the height was doubled to 10 inches.

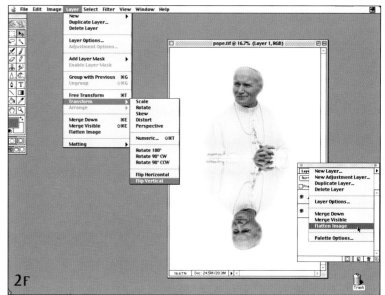

2F. The image was then rotated using **Layers›Transform›Flip Vertical**. The layer was dragged down to the bottom of the canvas with the arrow tool. Next, the layer was flattened using **Layer›Flatten Image** before new images of the Pope were added to the montage.

13

2G. To create a compressed image for the Pope montage, the size was changed in dimension by choosing **Image›Image Size**. While keeping the "Constrain Proportions" box unchecked, a new print size was entered in the dialog box.

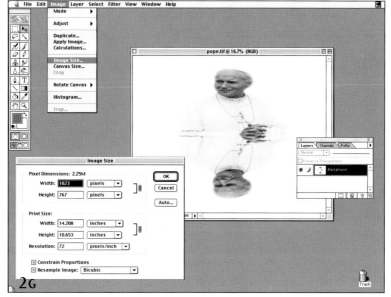

the gaussian blur in Adobe Photoshop allowed seamless pasting once all the "pope" images were pasted together.

virtual tips

creating layer 2

2H. A third image of the Pope was created for the montage. A copy of the original Pope image was pasted into a new layer by clicking the layer window. In **Layer › Layer Options**, the settings were adjusted to Multiply: 100%.

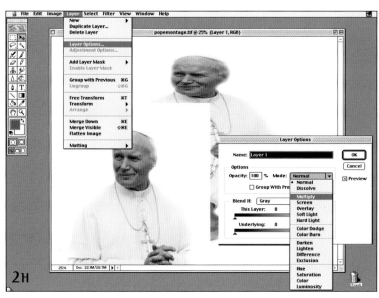

2H

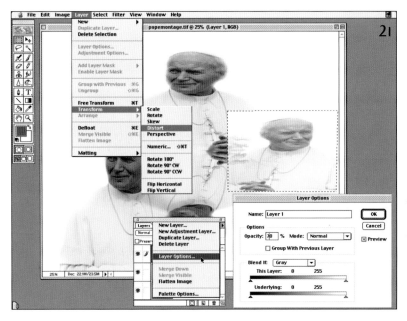

2I

2I. A fourth image of the Pope was created by pasting the original Pope picture into a new layer by clicking the layer window. It was then distorted by using **Layer › Transform › Distort**. To add further dimension to the layer of the montage, **Layer › Layer Options** was chosen and Opacity: 70% was added to the fourth Pope figure.

2J. To complete the montage within a montage, a final image was pasted by clicking the layer window. Then, **Layer › Transform › Scale** was applied, positioning the figure to the left of the montage and scaled to fit. The image was then flattened using **Layer › Flatten Image**. [⌘Command Key+A] and [⌘Command Key+C] were used to select and copy the area, respectively.

final image

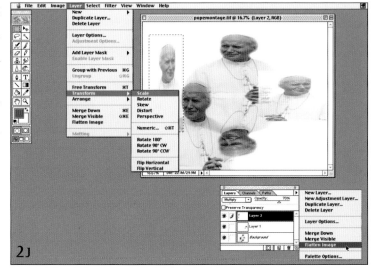

2J

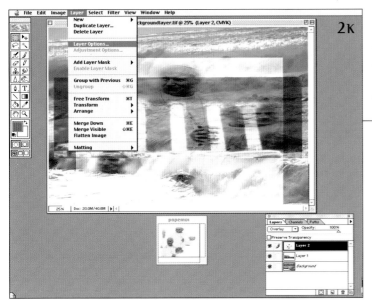

2K **2K.** In the original montage, a new layer of the Pope montage was pasted in by clicking the layer window. Layer 2 was finalized by using **Layer › Layer Options** and the dialog box was set at Opacity: 100%.

creating layer 3

3A. An antique photograph of a young girl's First Holy Communion was scanned and opened in Adobe Photoshop.

3A

3B

3B. Using **Layer › Transform › Scale**, the photo was elongated until the image covered only half the width of the canvas size. This was achieved by dragging the handle on the right side of the window.

3C. **Image › Adjust › Brightness/Contrast** was then used to fade the image into a translucent sepia tone. The settings were adjusted to Brightness: +15 and Contrast: -30.

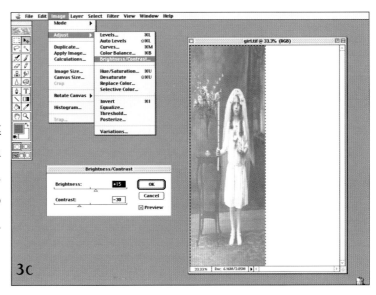

3C

creating layer 3

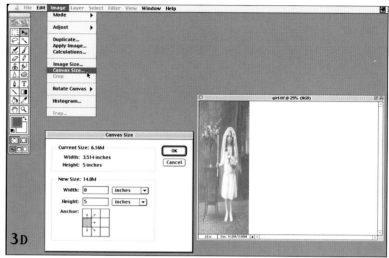

3D. The canvas size was adjusted to coincide with the image area of the background montage. Using **Image›Canvas Size**, the size was set to Width: 8 inches and Height: 5 inches.

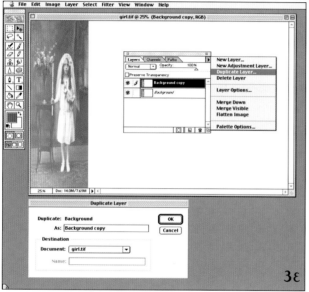

3ε. A duplicate image was made through commands in the Layers palette. **Layers›Duplicate Layer** was selected to make a background copy of the girl's First Communion image. The image was then grabbed with the arrow tool and slid to the right of the canvas screen.

3F. **Layer›Layer Options** was selected to activate the Layer Options dialog box. The Options were set at Opacity: 100% and Mode: Darken. **Layer›Transform›Flip Horizontal** was chosen to mirror the image on Layer 3. **Layer›Flatten Layer** was applied. [⌘ Command Key+A] was used to select the area, and [⌘ Command Key+C] was used to copy it.

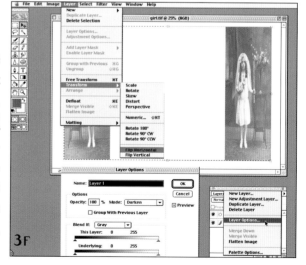

final image

VirtualMedia A Step-By-Step Techniques Guide

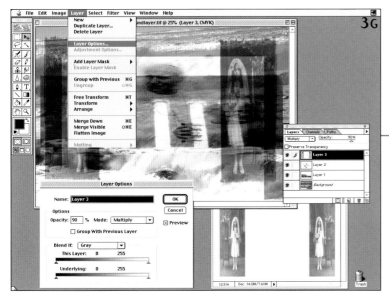

3G. The First Communion image was then added to the montage by using [⌘Command Key+V] to paste the new Layer 3. **Layer›Layer Options** activated the third Layer dialog box, and the Options were set at Opacity: 90% and Mode: Multiply.

creating
layer 4

4A. A stock image of an ancient Mexican pyramid was opened into Adobe Photoshop.

17

4B. Layer›Transform›Scale was used to create a narrow distorted image. The image was then compressed into the lower 1/3 of the canvas by pushing down on the top of the window handle. [⌘Command Key+A] was used to select and [⌘Command Key+C] was used to copy the area for the background montage.

4C. Layer›New›Layer dialog box was opened. Setting were adjusted to Opacity: 60% and Mode: Multiply. To finalize Layer 4, [⌘Command Key+V] was used to paste the pyramid image into the background montage.

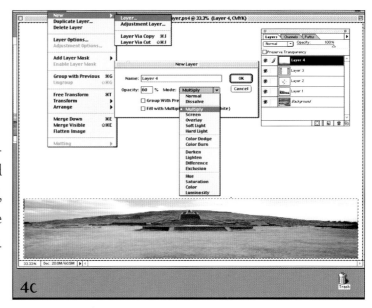

creating layer 5

5A. A vestige holy card was scanned into Adobe Photoshop.

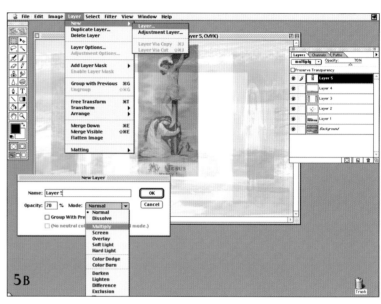

5B. [⌘Command Key+A] was used to select and [⌘Command Key+C] was used to copy the image. **Layer›New›Layer** was opened and the settings were adjusted to Opacity: 70% and Mode: Multiply. Layer 5 was pasted into place with [⌘Command Key+V].

creating layer 6

6A. A file of a Holy Card prayer was opened into Adobe Photoshop. [⌘Command Key+A] was used to select and [⌘Command Key+C] was used to copy the text.

6B. **Layer›New›Layer** was opened and Layer 6 settings were adjusted to Opacity: 70% and Mode: Overlay. The card was pasted into place with [⌘Command Key+V]. [⌘Command Key+I] was then used to invert the image.

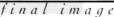

final image

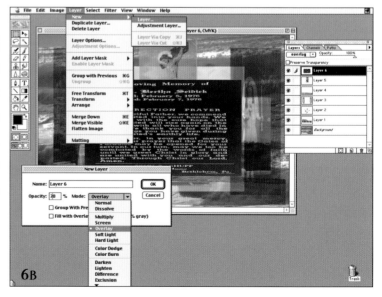

creating layer 7

7A. An old family photograph was scanned into Adobe Photoshop.

7B. [⌘Command Key+A] selected and [⌘Command Key+C] copied the image. **Layer › New › Layer** was opened, and Layer 7 settings were adjusted to Opacity: 70% and Mode: Hard Light. Layer 7 was then pasted into place using [⌘Command Key+V] to finalize the complete image.

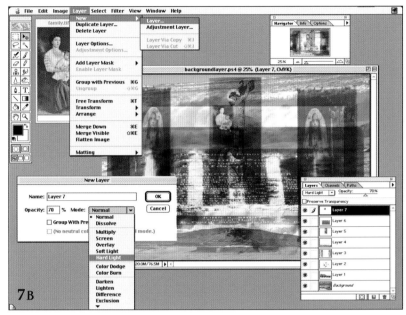

final image

A Step-By-Step Techniques Guide

VirtualMedia

Kumbum Chorten

PURPOSE sacred places series
DIGITAL CREATIVE lisa johnston
SOFTWARE adobe photoshop

San Geranimo

PURPOSE sacred places series
DIGITAL CREATIVE lisa johnston
SOFTWARE adobe photoshop

MOSQUE OF ZEINAB

PURPOSE sacred places series
DIGITAL CREATIVE lisa johnston
SOFTWARE adobe photoshop

Send

PURPOSE promotion
DIGITAL CREATIVE margaret carsello
CLIENT kaleidoscope imaging
SOFTWARE adobe photoshop

MargareT
CarseLLo

Margaret Carsello's design philosophy is not just

to look, but to see. What she can see, she can

then feel and create. Adobe Photoshop allows

her to combine her own drawings, paintings,

photographs, and collage into one medium that

is infinitely variable. Adobe Illustrator and

Adobe Dimensions are also part of her electronic

palette. Creating and understanding color is the

single most important aspect of her work, says

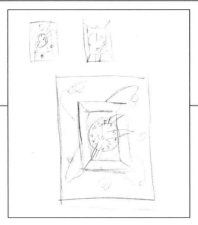

sketch

SKETCH. A few rough pencil sketches were created of the concept for reference.

creating the
background layer

A. An original painting was created using acrylics on paper.
The painting was scanned into Adobe Photoshop, where
Window›Layers was used to apply it as the Background Layer.

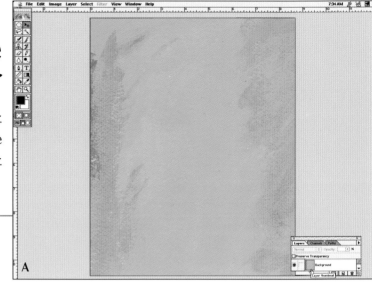

creating the
orbit layer

1A. An image from an astrology book was also scanned into Adobe Photoshop.
[⌘Command Key+A] selected and [⌘Command Key+C] copied the image.

VirtualMedia A Step-By-Step Techniques Guide

1B. The New Layer dialog box was
opened where the settings were
adjusted to Opacity: 78% and
Mode: Lighten. [⌘Command V]
pasted in the Orbit Layer.

final image

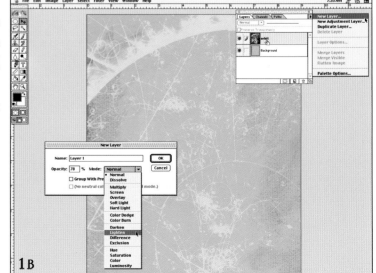

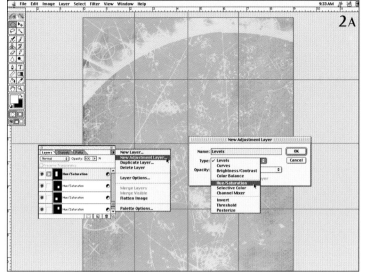

creating the hue/saturation layer

2A. Rules were aligned to create quadrant sections. Using the Marquee Tool, a section was selected. The **Layer›New Adjustment Layer** was opened. In the New Adjustment options box, Hue/Saturation was opened.

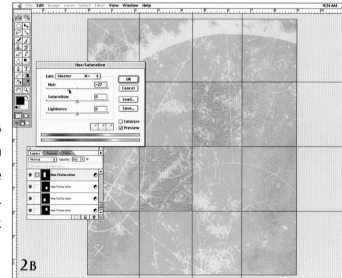

2B. In the Hue/Saturation box, the Hue slider was moved to the left for a setting of -27. The change in hue resulted in a dramatic color shift in the original green color of the quadrant. Two sections were altered in color.

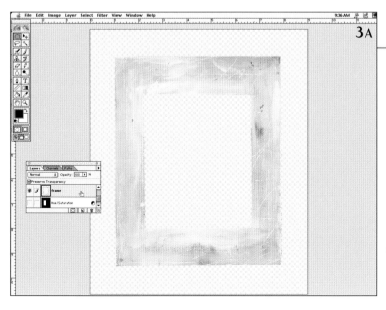

creating the frame layer

3A. An original acrylic painting was scanned on a flatbed and opened into Adobe Photoshop. [⌘Command Key+A] was used to select and [⌘Command Key+C] was used to copy the image. [⌘Command V] pasted in the Frame Layer.

the new adjustment layer in Adobe Photoshop 4.0 allows for a wide variety of effects to be applied to each layer underneath.

virtual tips

creating the orbit layer

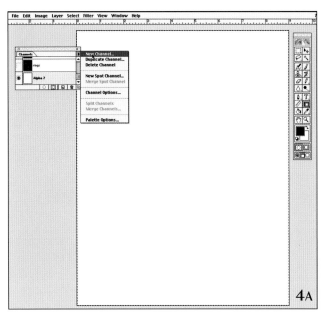

4A. A new channel was created by opening **Channel› New Channel** for the Orbit Rings Layer.

4B. Circular rings were created in Adobe Illustrator and imported into Adobe Photoshop. **File›Place** was opened, and the rings were loaded into the new channel. [Shift Key+⌘Command Key+D] was used to open the Feather Selection dialog box,

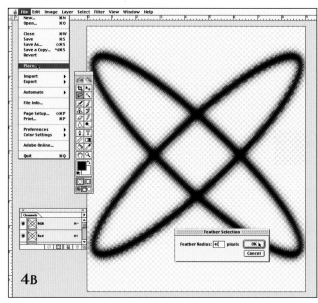

where the setting was adjusted to Feather Radius: 40 pixels.

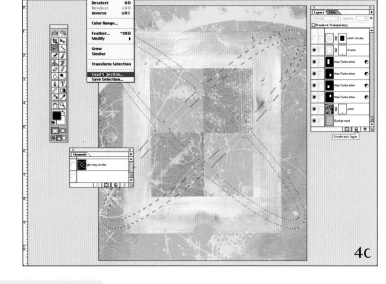

4C. The Create New Layers icon was clicked to make a new layer. The orbit circles channel was loaded. **Select›Load Selection** was implemented to load the image and finalize the Orbit Circles Layer.

4D. **Edit›Fill** was used to open the Fill dialog box and change the circle rings from black to orange.

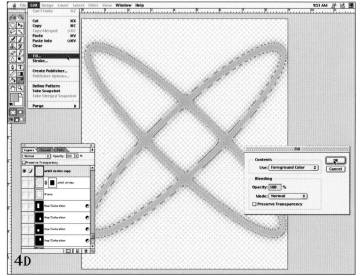

VirtualMedia *A Step-By-Step Techniques Guide*

final image

creating the
flower layer

5A. A stock photograph of a bird of paradise flower was imported into Adobe Photoshop. **Layer›Free Transform** was used to size the image to fit properly into the space.

creating the target layer

6A. An image of concentric circles was created in Adobe Illustrator and imported into Adobe Photoshop. **File›Place** was opened, and the circles were loaded into the new channel.

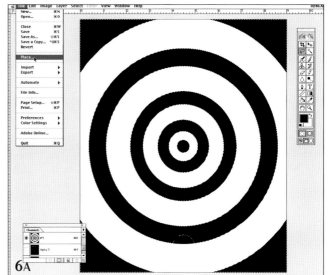

6A

6B. The circles were selected with the Lasso Tool. **Select›Load Selection** was used to save the selection as a new channel.

6B

6C. The New Adjustment Layer options box was opened from **Layer›New Adjustment Layer**. From there the Hue/Saturation dialog box was opened, and the sliders were set at Hue: +27, Saturation: +23 and Lightness: +5.

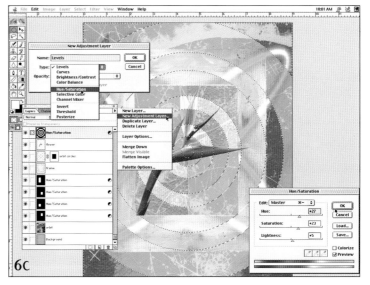

6C

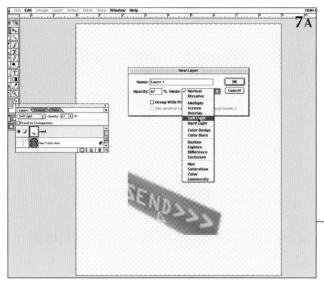

creating the send layer

7A. A digital image isolated from a stock photo was imported into Adobe Photoshop. It was then placed into the working file, and a new layer was made. The settings were adjusted to Opacity: 67% and Mode: Soft Light.

creating the planets and shell layer

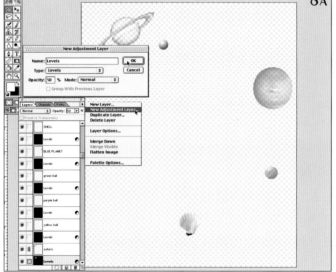

8A. Elements were imported into Adobe Photoshop and placed into the working file. New layers were made for each element by selecting **Layer › New Adjustment Layer**. In the New Adjustment Layer dialog box, the settings were adjusted to Opacity: 50% and Mode: Normal.

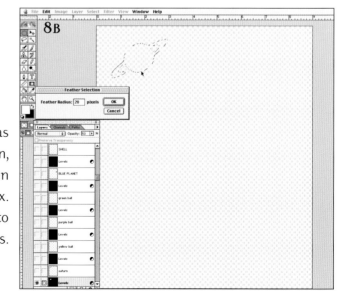

8B. In each layer, [⌘Control Key+A] was used to select every element. Then, [Shift+⌘Control Key+D] was used to open the Feather Selection dialog box. The settings were adjusted to Feather Radius: 20 pixels.

final image

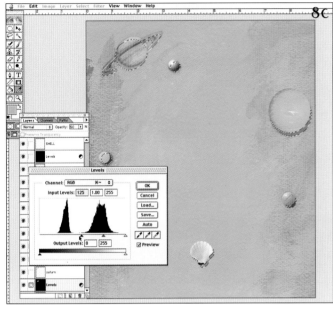

8C. The layers were pushed slightly to the right to create drop shadows. The shadows were selected using [⌘Command Key+A]. [⌘Command Key+L] was implemented to open the Levels dialog box. The sliders were then adjusted to create a darker area of pixels for the drop shadows.

creating the clock layer

9A. An old file from a previous project was opened in Adobe Photoshop. It was then placed in a new channel using **File›Place**.

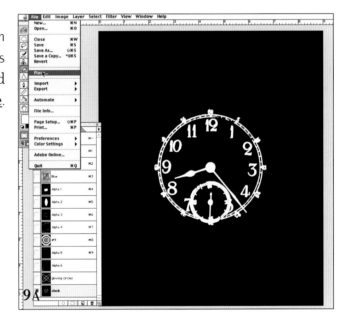

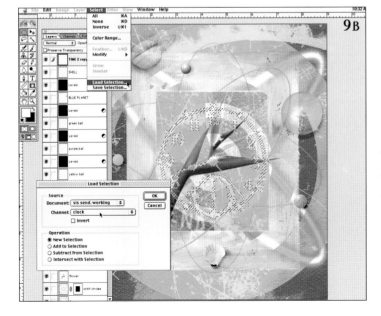

9B. The "Create New Layers" icon was clicked to make a new layer. The clock channel was then loaded. Using **Select›Load Selection**, the image was loaded into the channel.

9C. The selection was then filled with the foreground white color using **Edit› Fill.** The settings in the Fill dialog box were adjusted to Opacity: 40%.

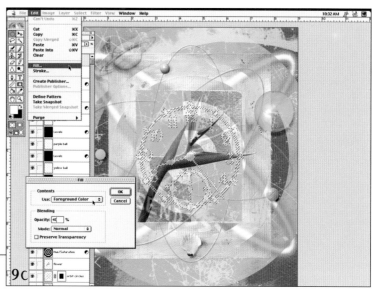

9C

final image

VirtualMedia A Step-By-Step Techniques Guide

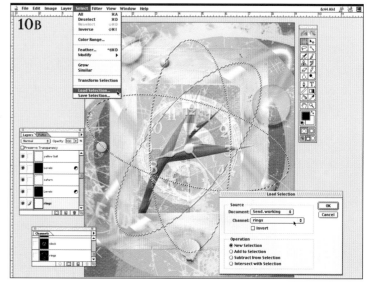

10A

creating the rings layer

10A. Circular rings created in Adobe Illustrator were opened in Adobe Photoshop. They were then placed in a new channel using **File› Place**.

10B. The "Create New Layers" icon was clicked to make a new layer. **Select› Load Selection** was implemented to load the rings channel.

10B

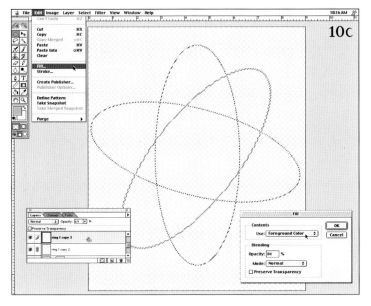

10C. The rings were filled with the foreground color using
Edit›Fill. The settings in the Fill dialog box were adjusted to
Opacity: 84%.

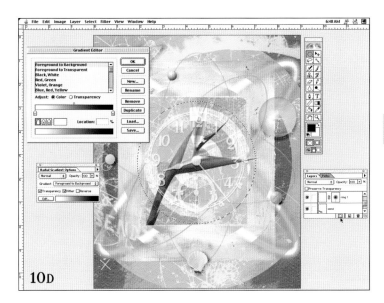

31

10D. The Mask icon in the Layers Palette was
clicked, and a circle was drawn with the
Ellipse Marquee Tool. The Gradient Tool was
double clicked to open the Options Palette.
After Edit was clicked, the Gradient Editor was
used to soften the center and finalize the image.

f i n a l   i m a g e

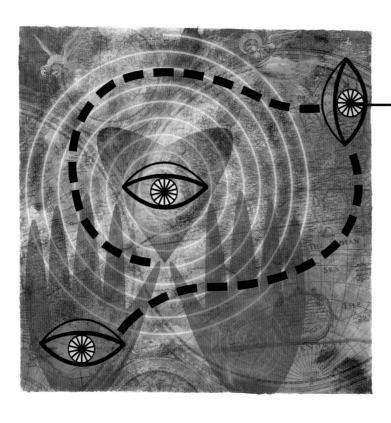

ATTRACTION

PURPOSE promotion
DIGITAL CREATIVE margaret carsello
CLIENT kaleidoscope imaging
SOFTWARE adobe photoshop

ITALIA

PURPOSE promotion
DIGITAL CREATIVE margaret carsello
SOFTWARE adobe photoshop

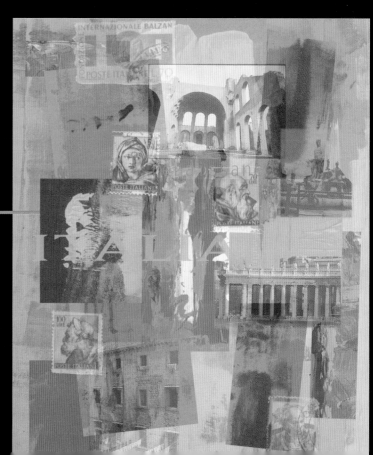

VIRGO

August 24 · September 22

I am the maiden, innocent of earthly pleasure,
tirelessly harvesting knowledge and sifting facts.
I know more of the ways of the intellect;
the rewards of work; the satisfaction in serving.
I have a way with wit and with words—
the vanguard of information in its age.
I am a sentinel for the purity of this planet
and the wellness of its inhabitants;
I make order out of chaos for a better world.

VIRGO

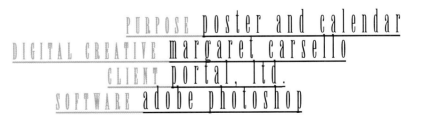

PURPOSE poster and calendar
DIGITAL CREATIVE margaret carsello
CLIENT portal, ltd.
SOFTWARE adobe photoshop

Clown

PURPOSE cd promotion

DIGITAL CREATIVE scott petty

CLIENT bee hive design co.

SOFTWARE adobe photoshop

SCOTT PETTY

Scott Petty strives to keep his distressed collages

free from artificial human conventions like time

and literalism. Instead, he is more interested in the

duration of emotions, a world in which borders are not

as well defined. Petty's dream-like collages begin as

sketches and found objects: He must touch everything

before restructuring it in Adobe Photoshop and

Illustrator. Poetry, medicine, modern art, machinery,

history, cartography, and even the "beauty of decay"

sketch

SKETCH. A quick concept sketch was created
in the form of a collage from cut Polaroids,
ink, children's paints and a paper plate.

creating the
background layer

A. An old family photograph was scanned
into Adobe Photoshop.

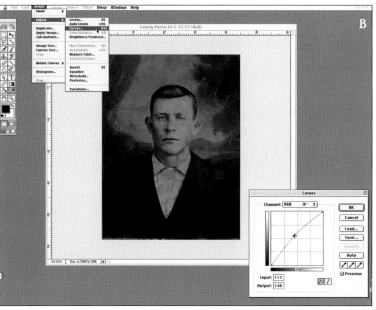

B. The image was color
corrected by opening
Image›Adjust›Curves.
To adjust the color values in
the highlights, shadows and
mid-tones, the crossbar was
dragged slightly off center.

C. The image was then saved as
a Background Layer by using
Window›Show Layers.

final image

creating layer 1

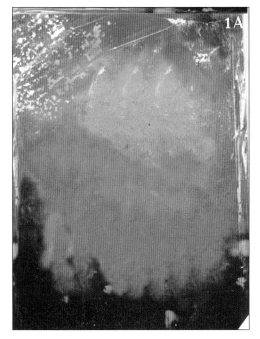

1A. From his extensive library of hand-painted textures, he scanned this painting into Adobe Photoshop.

1B. [⌘Command Key+A] selected and **Edit›Copy** was used to copy the image area.

1C. **Layer›New›Layer** was opened, and the settings were adjusted to Opacity: 30% and Mode: Overlay. Layer 1 was activated with the Move Tool and **Edit›Paste** was implemented to paste the layer.

≈∞ Using the layer palette Layers Options, allows for unlimited design flexibility in the creative process.

virtual tips

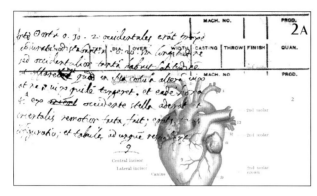

creating layer 2

2A. Three printed transparencies were superimposed together on the flatbed and scanned as black and white line art.

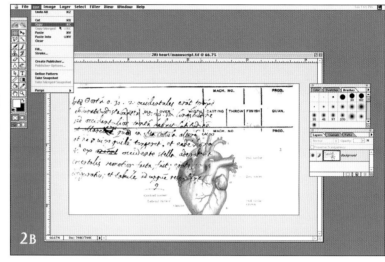

2B. [⌘Command Key+A] selected and **Edit›Copy** copied the image area.

final image

VirtualMedia A Step-By-Step Techniques Guide

2C. **Layer›New›Layer** was opened, and the settings were adjusted to Opacity: 100% and Mode: Lighten. Layer 2 was activated with the Move Tool and [⌘Command Key+V] pasted in the new layer.

2D. The heart image was then reversed using **Select›Inverse**.

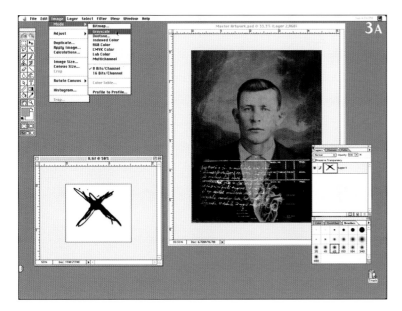

creating layer 3

3A. An "x" was scribed with India ink. The image was scanned and opened in Adobe Photoshop. It was changed to grayscale using **Image›Mode›Grayscale**.

3B. **Image›Mode›Duotone** was opened. Settings in the Duotone Options dialog box were adjusted to Type: Monotone and the color was changed to Pantone 1797.

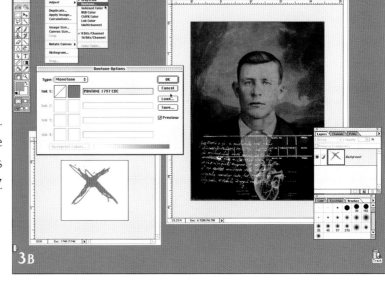

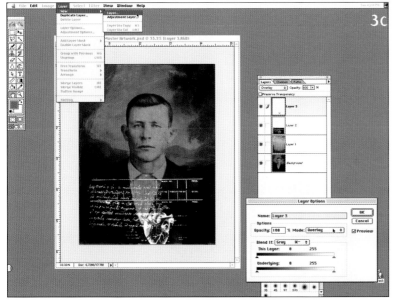

3C. [⌘Command Key+A] was used to select and [⌘Command Key+C] was used to copy the image area. **Layer›New›Layer** was activated. In the Layer Options dialog box, Layer 3 was set at Opacity: 100% and Mode: Overlay. Layer 3 was made active in the Layers Palette with the Move Tool, and [⌘Command Key+V] was applied to paste the "x" into the layer.

creating layer 4

4A. A hat image previously created for an experimental project was opened in Adobe Photoshop. The Eraser Tool was used to remove some of the hard edges while still keeping the collage style. [⌘Command Key+A] was used to select the image area, and **Edit›Copy** was used to copy the image area.

4B. **Layer›New ›Layer** was activated. In the Layer 4 Options dialog box, the settings remained at Opacity: 100% and Mode: Normal. Layer 4 was made active in the Layers Palette with the Move Tool, and [⌘Command Key+V] pasted in the layer.

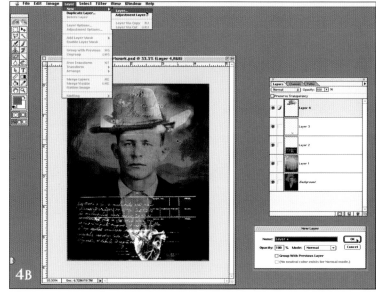

VirtualMedia A Step-By-Step Techniques Guide

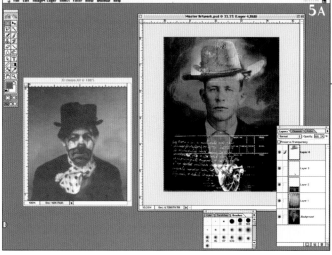

creating layer 5

5A. An old family photo of a clown was scanned and imported into Adobe Photoshop.

5B. With the Marquee Tool, an area of the clown was selected. **Image›Adjust›Auto Levels** was used to adjust the contrast. [⌘Command Key+A] was used to select and [⌘Command Key+C] was used to copy the image area.

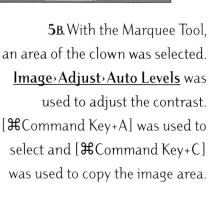

final image

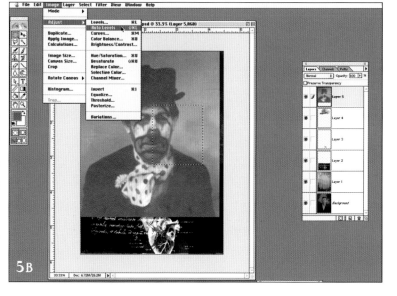

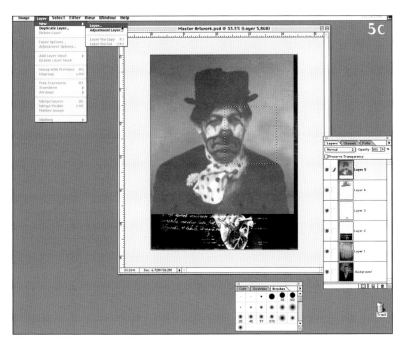

5C. **Layer›New›Layer** was activated. Layer 5 was made active in the Layers Palette with the Move Tool, and [⌘Command Key+V] was used to paste in the layer.

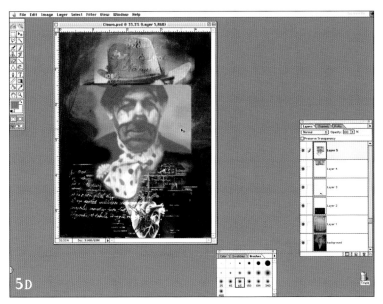

5D. Using the Eraser Tool, the background and other areas were removed. The image was finalized by using the Pen and Eraser Tools to add free-form drawing and scratches.

f i n a l   i m a g e

ANALOG

PURPOSE cd cover
DIGITAL CREATIVE scott petty
CLIENT bee hive design co.
SOFTWARE adobe photoshop

ANALOG No.2

PURPOSE promotion
DIGITAL CREATIVE scott petty
CLIENT bee hive design co.
SOFTWARE adobe photoshop

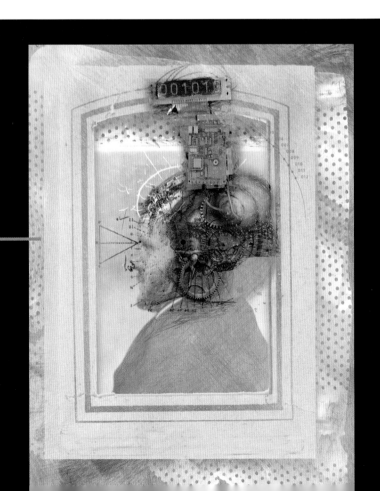

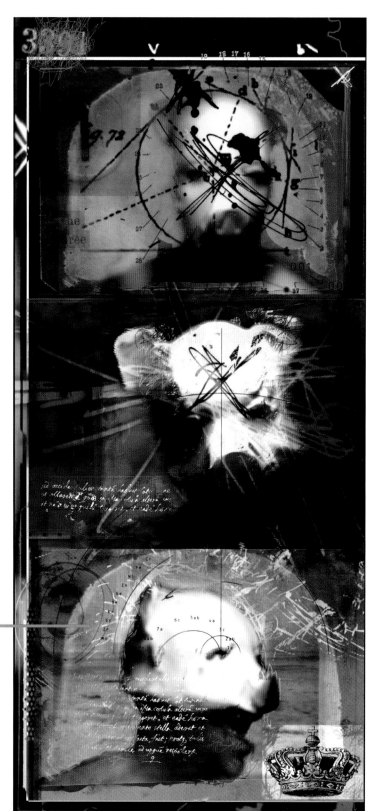

3 PIGS

PURPOSE book
DIGITAL CREATIVE scott petty
CLIENT old pike
SOFTWARE adobe photoshop

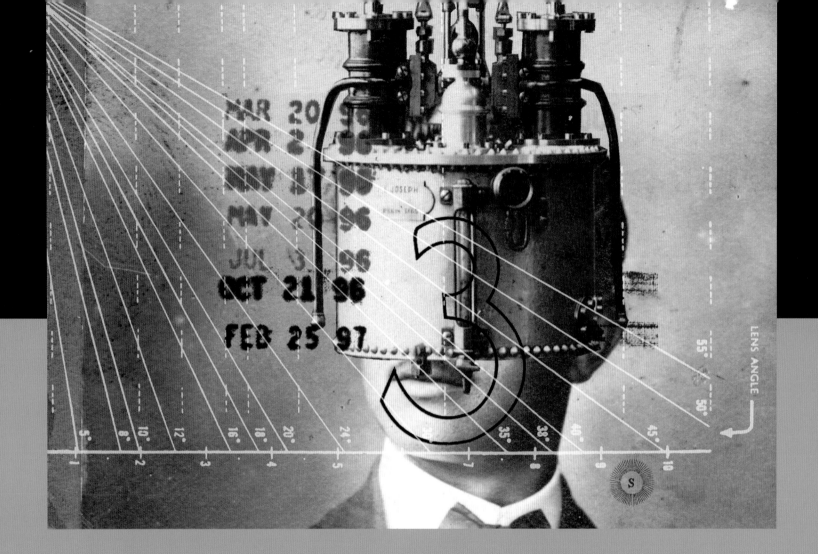

SPANISH MAN

PURPOSE promotion
DIGITAL CREATIVE jason statts
SOFTWARE adobe photoshop

Jason
Howard Statts

Everything from the work of other artists to painted

walls and rotting cardboard boxes inspires Jason

Howard Statts. The artist does not want his distressed

collages to look like digital imagery, but admits that

this is sometimes impossible: The multi-layered mix

creating layer 1

1A. A photograph of a Spanish man was scanned and opened in Adobe Photoshop. The area was selected with the Marquee Tool and copied with **Edit›Copy**.

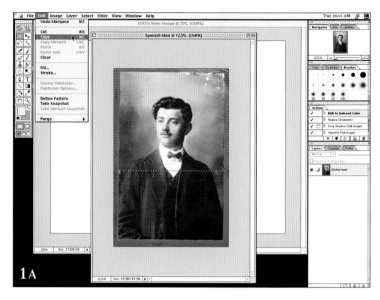

1B. The image of the man was then pasted into the working canvas to make Layer 1, using [⌘Command Key+V]. **Layer›Transform›Scale** was used to scale the image to fit the canvas.

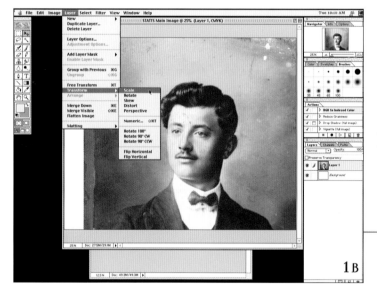

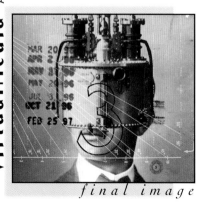

final image

creating layer 2

2A. An existing file of an old helicopter motor was opened in Adobe Photoshop. The Lasso Tool was used to remove the background area. The image was then selected with the Marquee Tool and copied using **Edit›Copy**.

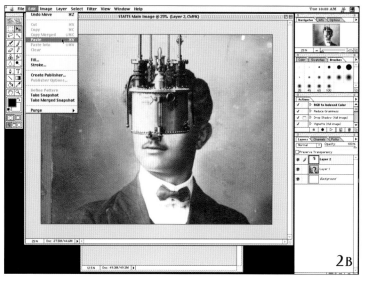

2B. To complete Layer 2, **Edit › Paste**
was used to paste the motor into the
working canvas.

2C. <u>Layer › Transform › Scale</u> was used
to size the motor image, by
dragging the window handles.

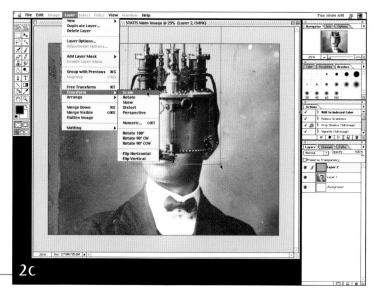

47

creating layer 3

3A. An old library check-out card was
scanned and opened into Adobe Photoshop.
The area was selected with the Marquee Tool
and copied.

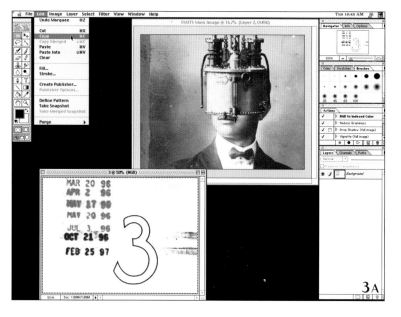

*Statts'
favorite tool is
the Lasso Tool.
It gives his
images a
"cut-out" look.*

virtual tips

3B. [⌘Command Key + V] pasted the library card into the working canvas to complete Layer 3. **Layers›Darken** was then applied in the Layers Palette to make the library card transparent.

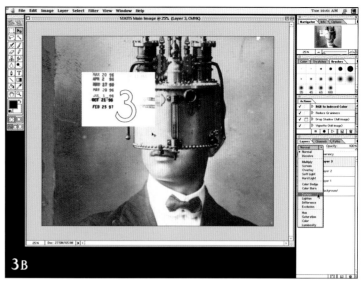

3B

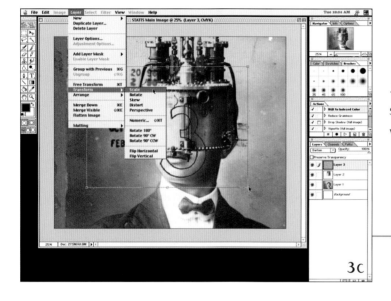

3C

3C. Layer›Transform›Scale was used to size the library card image by dragging the window handles.

creating layer 4

4A. A chart from a television video manual was scanned and opened in Adobe Photoshop. The area was selected with the Marquee Tool and copied.

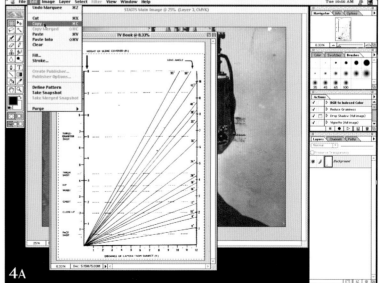

4A

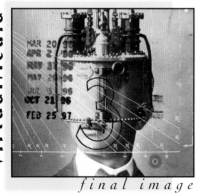

final image

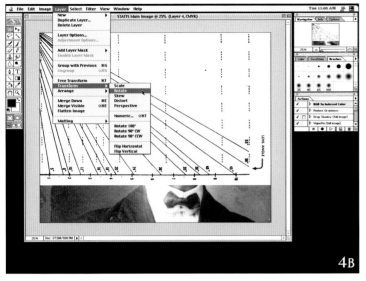

4B. [⌘Command Key + V] pasted the image into the working canvas to complete Layer 4. It was then rotated 90% using **Layer›Transform›Rotate**.

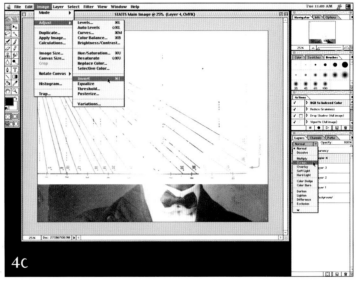

4C. The rotated image was then inverted using **Image›Adjust›Invert**. A screen was applied using **Layers›Screen** in the layers palette.

49

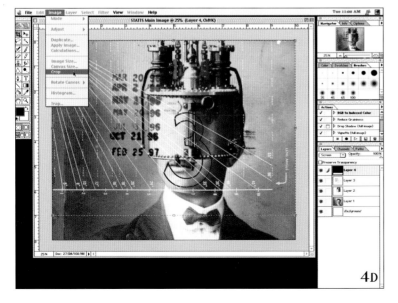

4D. The image was then cropped with **Image›Crop** to adjust the design.

creating layer 5

5A. A new layer was added for a solid color by clicking the Layers Icon in the Layers Palette.

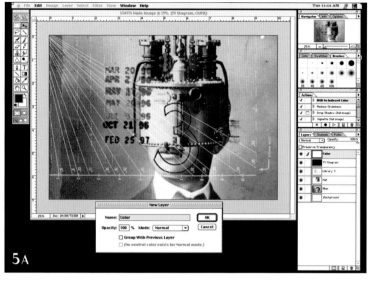

5A

5B. In the Color Picker dialog box, a bright blue was chosen for the solid color.

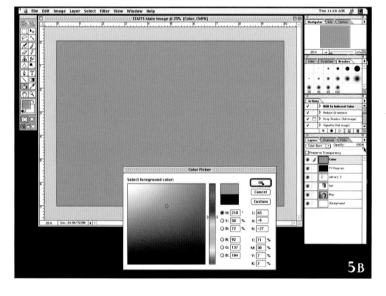

5B

5C. The blue was added to the color layer using the Paintbucket Tool. Then, using **Layers›Color Burn**, the blue tone was enhanced on the image.

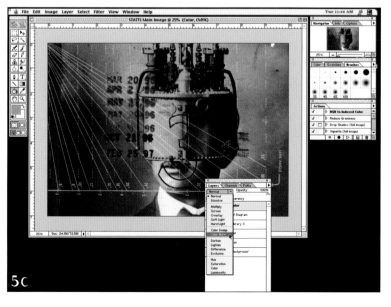

5C

final image

VirtualMedia A Step-By-Step Techniques Guide

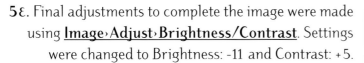

5D. In the Layers Palette, the opacity of the blue layer was reduced from 100% to 43%, using the slider, to create a more even color.

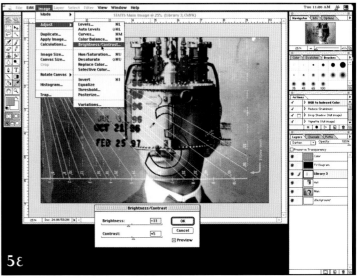

5E. Final adjustments to complete the image were made using **Image › Adjust › Brightness/Contrast**. Settings were changed to Brightness: -11 and Contrast: +5.

51

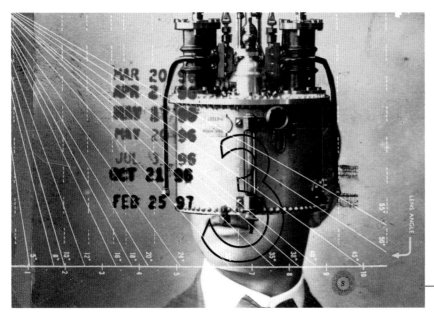

final image

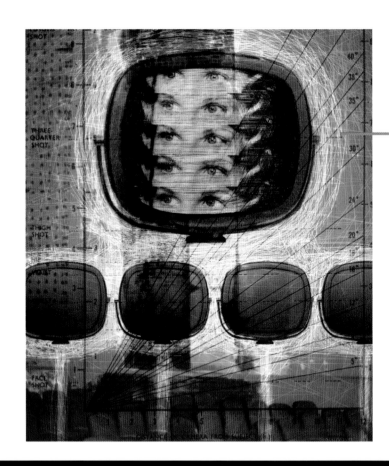

Re-Run Blues

PURPOSE editorial illustration
DIGITAL CREATIVE jason statts
CLIENT internet underground magazine
SOFTWARE adobe photoshop

Jazziz CD Cover

PURPOSE cd cover
DIGITAL CREATIVE jason statts
CLIENT jazziz magazine
SOFTWARE adobe photoshop

SUCH SIMPLE
MACHINES

PURPOSE record cover
DIGITAL CREATIVE jason statts
CLIENT dragbody
SOFTWARE adobe photoshop

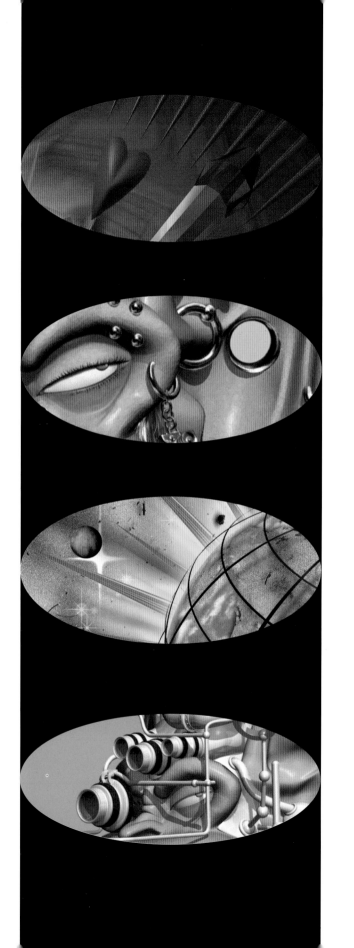

3D MODELING

Three-dimensional modeling is an artistic arena in which

digital illustration excels. With programs such as Ray

Dream Designer and Expression Tools Shade, artists can

build 3D structures, simulate depth, and suggest

dimension. The featured artists create simple lines that

FOREVER

PURPOSE background for skateboard ad
DIGITAL CREATIVE tony klassen
CLIENT flexdex
SOFTWARE ray dream designer & adobe photoshop

TONY
KLASSEN

Artist Tony Klassen wants his computer imagery

to fall into a category all its own, separate from

what everyone else is doing. Klassen's 3D modeled

images contain many photographs, each perfectly

blended into the main visual with the help of

sketch

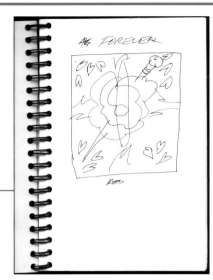

SKETCH. A pencil layout was drawn to determine which elements would be rendered in 3D.

creating the 3D elements

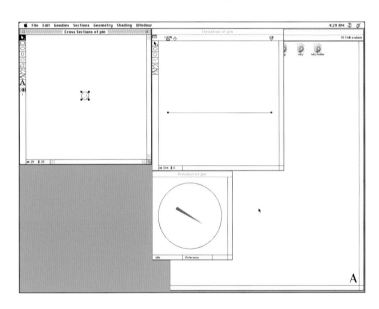

A. In Ray Dream Designer, a line was drawn in the Light Forge program. To create the Pin model, the slider arrow was clicked at 0% and 100% in the Elevation Window. This element was the basis for the Pin Frame, Heart Skewer, 3D Pin and Heart.

B. In the Scene Builder, multiple pins were assembled on a circular plane to create the Pin Frame.

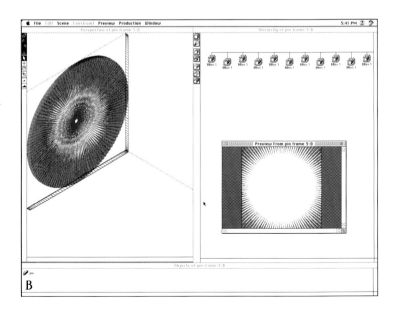

VirtualMedia A Step-By-Step Techniques Guide

final image

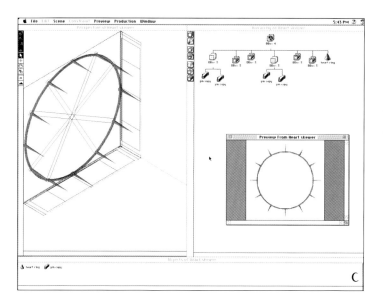

C. To create the Heart Ring, the pins were positioned around a 3D ring. As each part of the heart skewer was assembled, it was dragged to the Hierarchy Window and saved.

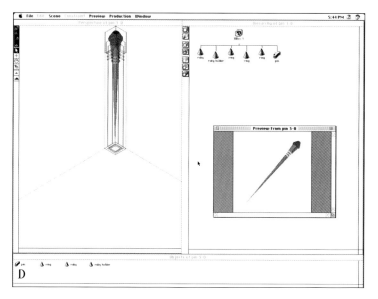

D. The construction of the 3D Pin representing a scepter was fabricated from three rings and a geometric shape for the ruby gemstone.

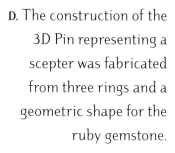

ε. The model of the heart was made into a narrower 3D shape by dragging the corner of the box in the Perspective Window.

Using Ray Dream Designer, each part of the model can be dragged into the Hierarchy window and saved for future experimenting.

virtual tips

creating the background layer

1A. An existing file of a colorful background pattern was imported into Adobe Photoshop. [⌘Command Key+A] selected and [⌘Command Key+C] copied each section into the working canvas. The patterns were turned using **Image›Rotate Canvas›...** and pasted into each layer using [⌘Command Key+V].

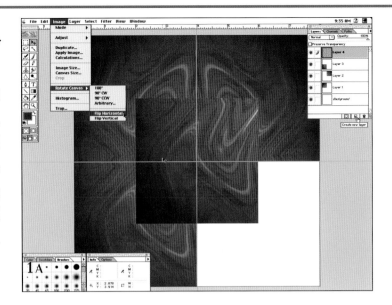

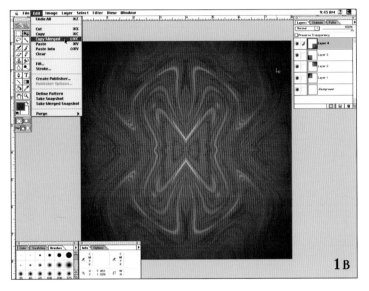

1B. Once the elements were in place, the patterns created a kaleidoscope effect. **Edit›Copy Merged** was then applied to rejoin them into one layer.

V i r t u a l M e d i a A Step-By-Step Techniques Guide

1C. The image was twisted using the **Filter›Distort›Twirl** at 999%.

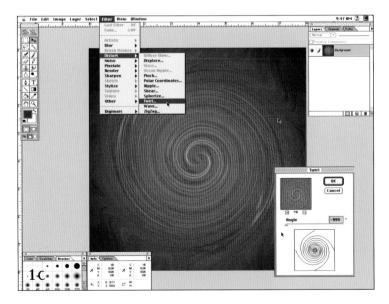

final image

creating the pin frame layer

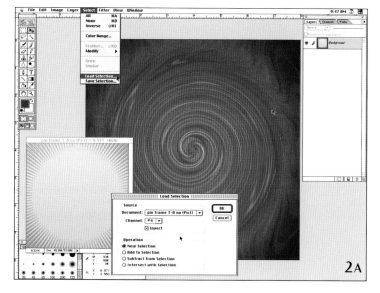

2A. The Pin Frame created in Ray Dream Designer, was imported into Adobe Photoshop, and the new image was loaded using **Select›Load Selection**.

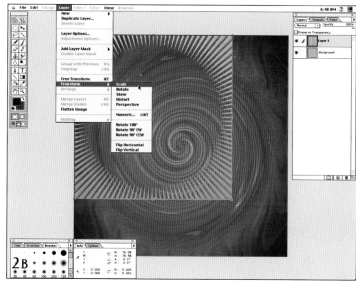

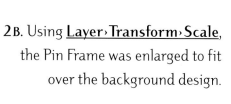

2B. Using **Layer›Transform›Scale**, the Pin Frame was enlarged to fit over the background design.

61

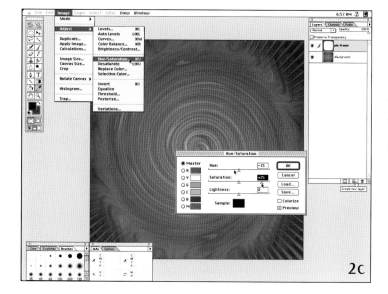

2C. **Image›Adjust›Hue/Saturation** was opened, and the sliders were adjusted to shift the color.

creating the heart skewer layer

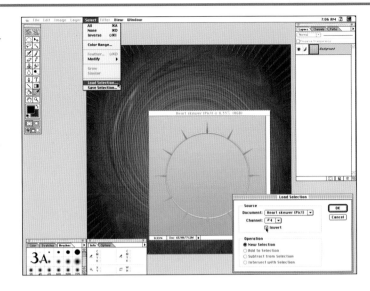

3A. The Heart Skewer created in Ray Dream Designer was imported into Adobe Photoshop, and the new image was loaded using **Select›Load Selection**.

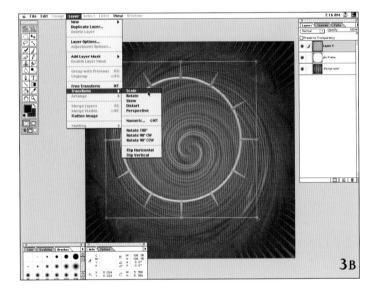

3B. Using **Layer›Transform›Scale**, the Heart Skewer was enlarged to fit over the area.

3C. Image›Adjust›Hue/Saturation was opened, and the sliders were adjusted to shift the color.

final image

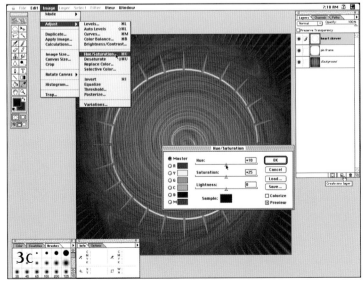

creating the fire layer

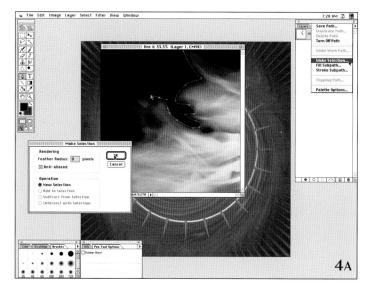

4A. A photograph of fire was opened in Adobe Photoshop. Using the Pen Tool, the flame was outlined. In the Path Palette, a new selection was made by opening Make Selection.

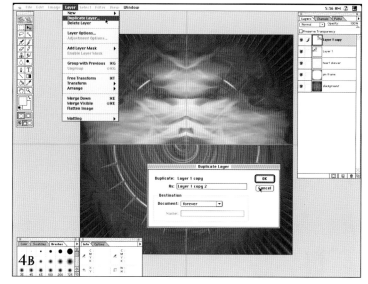

4B. A duplicate layer was made using **Layer›Duplicate Layer** for each fire segment. [⌘Command Key+A] selected and [⌘Command Key+C] copied each section. [⌘Command+V] pasted each area into the duplicate layer. **Image›Rotate Canvas** was applied to turn the position of the fire.

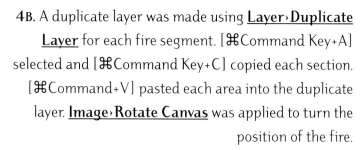

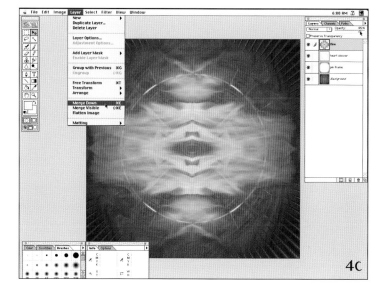

4C. Once in place, the sections were merged using **Layer›Merge Down**.

creating the heart skewer copy layer

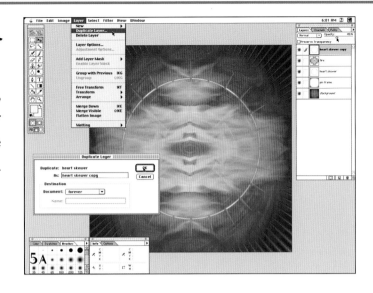

5A. Using **Layer›Duplicate Layer**, another layer of the Heart Skewer Layer was created. The opacity in the Layers Palette was adjusted to 45%.

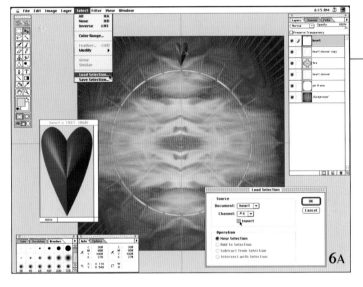

creating the heart layer

6A. The Heart created in Ray Dream Designer was imported into Adobe Photoshop, and the new image was loaded using **Select›Load Selection**. It was copied and pasted in the 12:00 position.

6B. Layer›Duplicate Layer was opened to make the Heart Copy Layer. The image was inverted and placed at the 6:00 position.

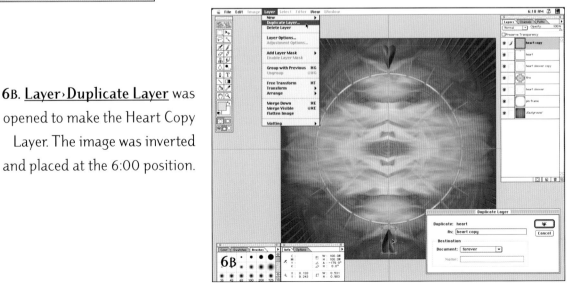

VirtualMedia A Step-By-Step Techniques Guide

final image

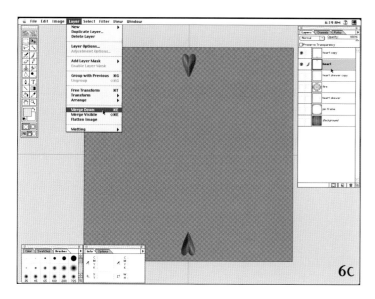

6C. Using **Layer › Merge Down**, the two heart layers were merged into one layer. [⌘Command Key+A] selected and [⌘Command Key+C] copied the heart section.

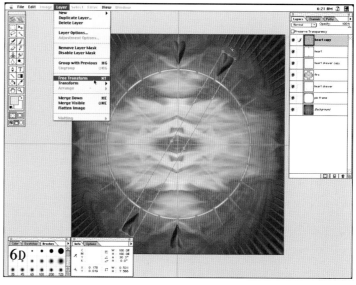

6D. 6E. [⌘Command+V] pasted each segment into place. Using **Layer › Free Transform** the section were rotated and positioned along the heart skewer ring.

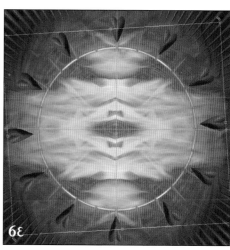

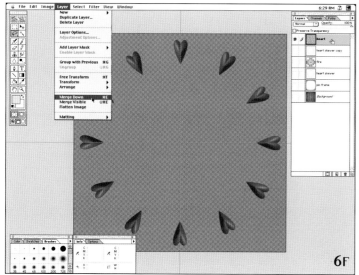

6F. Using **Layer › Merge Down**, all of the heart segments were merged into one layer.

creating the heart shadow layer

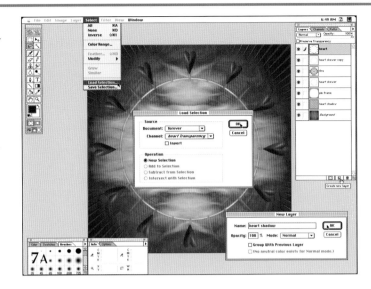

7A. A new layer, heart shadow, was made by clicking the Layers Icon in the Layers Palette window. **Select › Load Selection** loaded the image into the channel.

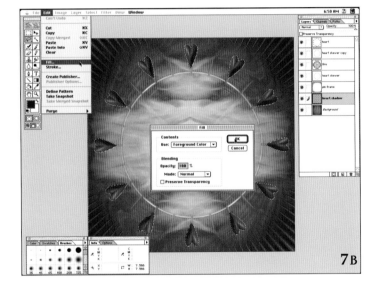

7B. Using **Edit › Fill**, the heart sections were filled with the foreground color.

7C. Using **Layer › Transform › Scale**, the Hearts were shifted to create a drop shadow effect.

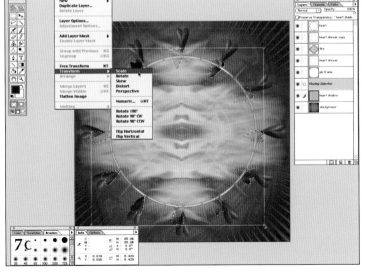

final image

VirtualMedia A Step-By-Step Techniques Guide

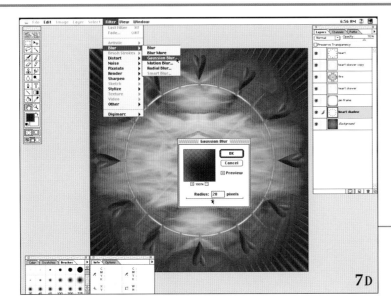

7D. **Filter›Blur›Gaussian Blur** was applied, with a Radius of 20 Pixels.

creating the poinsettia layer

8A. A photograph of a poinsettia was imported into Adobe Photoshop. The poinsettia was then outlined with the pen tool . **Make Path›** was activated in the Path Windows palette. [⌘Command+C] copied the image.

67

8B. A new layer for the poinsettia was opened by applying **Layer›New›Layer**. [⌘Command+V] pasted the image into the layer.

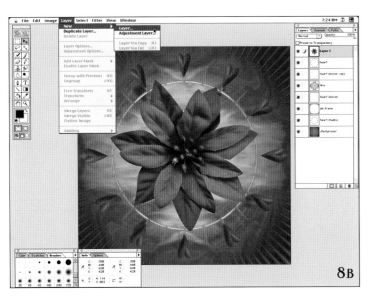

creating the fire edge layer

9A. A new channel was opened using the Channel Window. In the Path Windows, the Work Path was activated. Following the outline of the poinsettia as a guide , the edge was airbrushed in white.

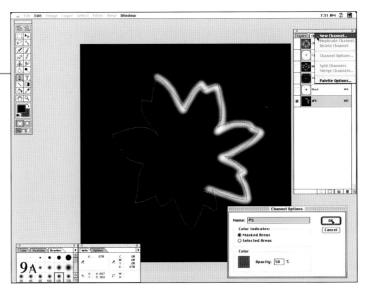

creating the fire edge layer

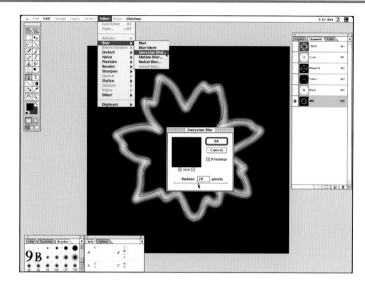

9B. <u>**Filter › Blur › Gaussian Blur**</u>
was applied, with a Radius
of 20 Pixels.

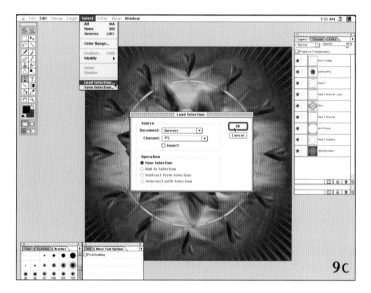

9C. <u>**Select › Load Selection**</u> was chosen. [⌘Command+C]
copied the Fire Layer. The Poinsettia Layer was clicked.
[⌘Command+V] pasted the Fire Edge Layer on top of the
poinsettia. The opacity was adjusted to 85%.

creating the pin layer

10A. The 3D Pin created in
Ray Dream Designer was imported
into Adobe Photoshop, and the
new image was loaded using
<u>**Select › Load Selection**</u>.
The opacity was adjusted to 85%.

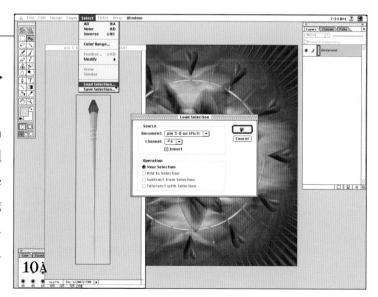

final image

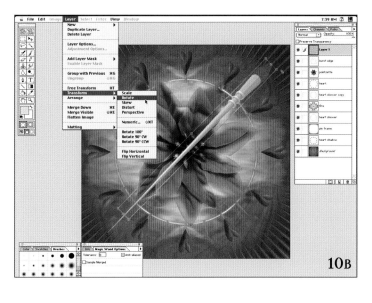

10B. Using **Layer›Transform›Rotate**, the 3D Pin was enlarged to fit across the poinsettia.

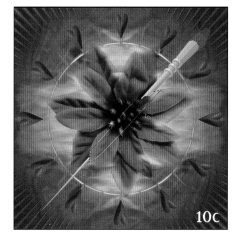

10C. A section of the poinsettia was outlined with the pen tool. [⌘Command+C] copied and [⌘Command+V] pasted the piece over the 3D pin.

69

f i n a l   i m a g e

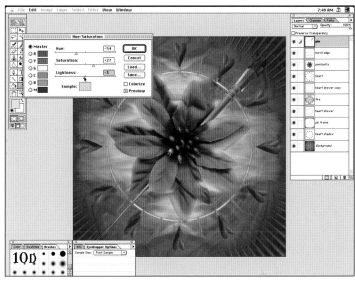

10D. Image›Adjust›Hue/Saturation was opened and the sliders were adjusted slightly.

A Step-By-Step Techniques Guide

EARTH WIND FIRE

PURPOSE album cover
DIGITAL CREATIVE tony klassen
CLIENT sony music
SOFTWARE ray dream designer
and adobe photoshop

VirtualMedia

AGELESS

PURPOSE background for skateboard ad
DIGITAL CREATIVE tony klassen
CLIENT flexdex skateboards
SOFTWARE ray dream designer
& adobe photoshop

ETERNAL

PURPOSE background for skateboard ad
DIGITAL CREATIVE tony klassen
CLIENT flexdex skateboards
SOFTWARE ray dream designer & adobe photoshop

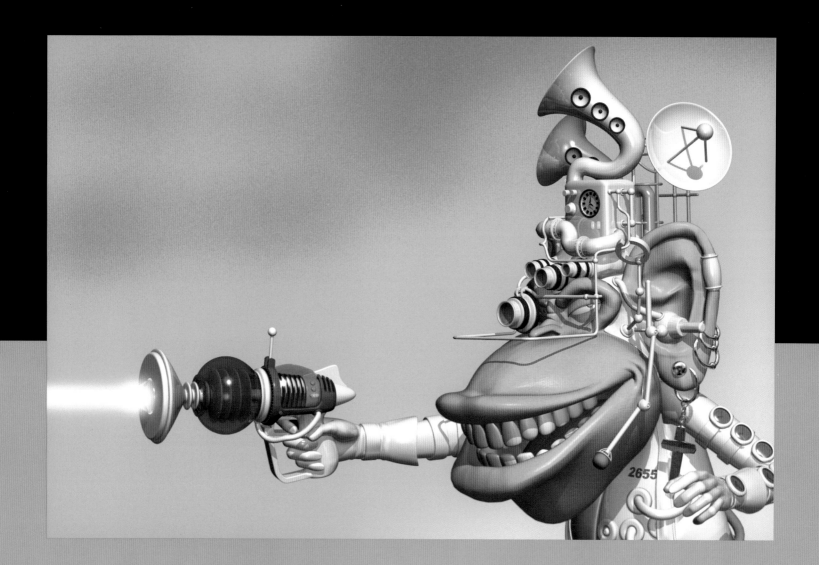

Ray Gun

PURPOSE advertisement
DIGITAL CREATIVE yasutaka taga
CLIENT zeex tenjin
SOFTWARE shade and adobe photoshop

YASUTAKA TAGA

Two powerful programs make Yasutaka Taga's eerily

realistic work possible-Adobe Photoshop and Expression

Tools' Shade. Taga uses Shade to give the art its

3D modeling shape, then opens Adobe Photoshop for

rendering. Photoshop is then used for texture mapping,

creating the head

1A. In Expression Tools' Shade, a line was drawn using **Tools›Pen›Open Line**. **Tools›Solid›Revolve** was opened to revolve a shape around the line to create a solid form for the head.

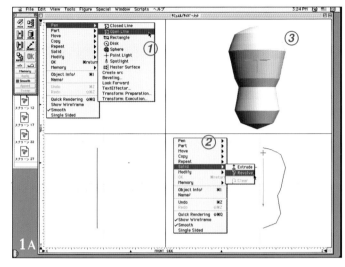

1B. From the Convert menu, a simple structured wireframe was applied. **Move›Rotate** allowed the form to revolve around itself to create a defined 3D shape.

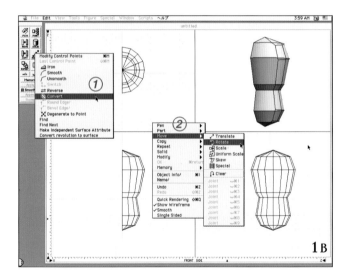

final image

VirtualMedia A Step-By-Step Techniques Guide

1C. Detail of the evolution of the construction of the head in the wireframe mode. The mouse was dragged over the surface to achieve the delineation of the facial structure.

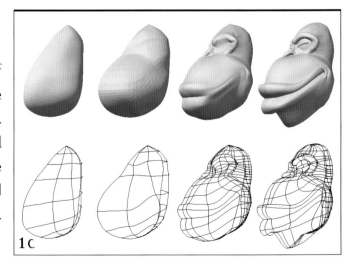

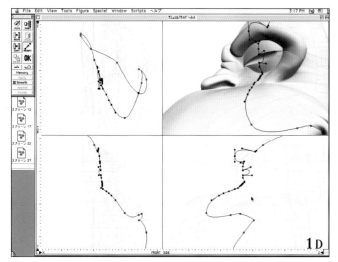

1 D. Since the surface wrinkles easily, the head was smoothed by working in wireframe mode. **Tools › Modify › Smooth** was opened. [⌘ Command+Space] was used to zoom in on particular areas. The points and lines were dragged to refine and smooth the face.

1 ε. [⌘ Command+Option+Space] was used to zoom out and review the work in progress. The transformation window was opened, and the x axis was changed to rotate the image.

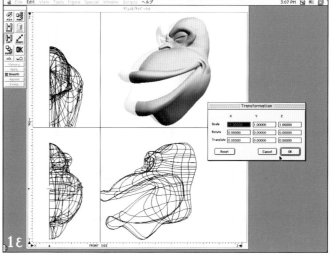

75

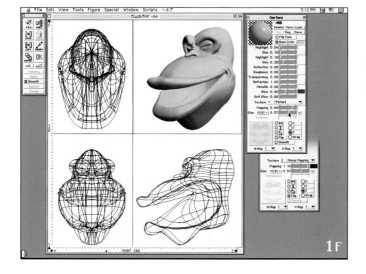

1 F. In the Surface dialog box, the sphere was rotated to indicate the light source. The base color box was checked to color the modeled head.

᠊᠊᠊ɷ In Shade, it is helpful to have the orthogonal view window screen open to see the model in all three angles as it develops.

virtual tips

creating the ear

2A. A base flat view of the ear was drawn. The mouse was then dragged across the x and y axis using [⌘Command+Option] keys to define the surface characteristics.

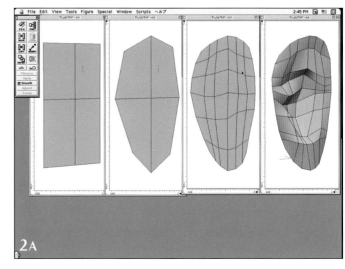

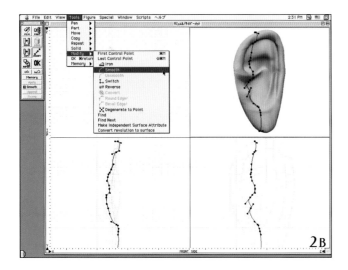

2B. **Tools›Modify›Smooth** was opened to refine and smooth the surface areas. Using the mouse, the points were dragged slightly until the shape was flowing and uniform.

VirtualMedia A Step-By-Step Techniques Guide

final image

2C. The inside of the ear (180°) was made first. Next, the outside of the ear was made by duplicating and remodeling it.

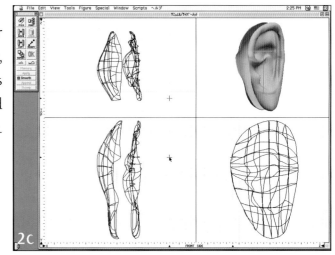

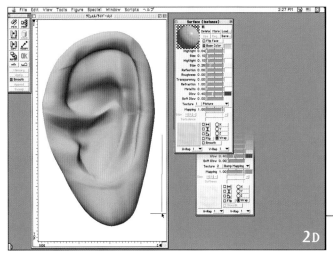

2D. In the Surface dialog box, the sphere was rotated to indicate the light source. The base color box was checked to color the modeled ear.

creating the body

3A. A body was made in the same method as the head. **Tools›Solid›Revolve** was opened to revolve a shape around the line, to create a solid form for the body. From the Convert menu, a simple structured wireframe was applied.

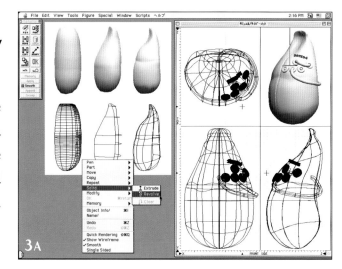

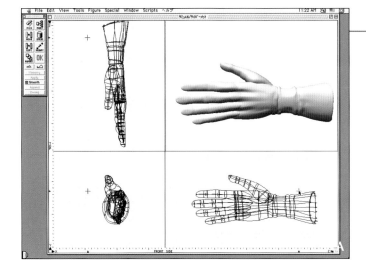

creating the hand

4A. The hand was constructed from six objects; the palm and fingers. The mouse was dragged to elongate the fingers to the desired extension.

creating the arm

5A. From the shoulder to the wrist, the arm was made from one curved, modeled shape. The rotator joint was placed at the shoulder and elbow. The watch was created from four elements. Six of them were placed on the arm.

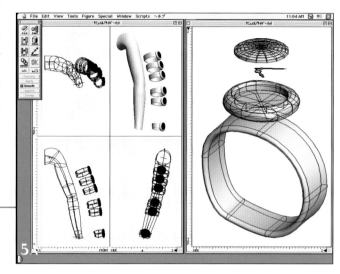

creating the legs and feet

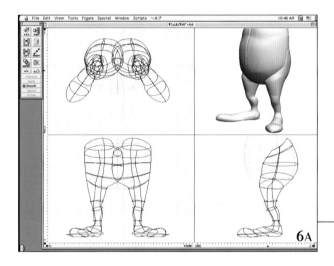

6A. The legs and feet were formed from one modeled shape. It was then attached to the body model.

creating the trousers

7A. The trousers were made by using cylindrical shapes for the openings in the legs and body.

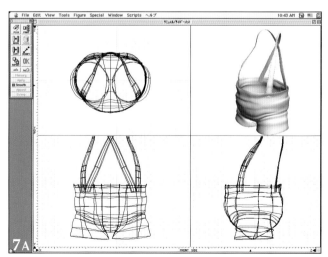

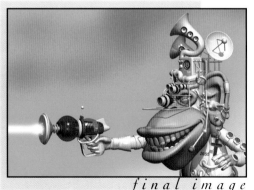

final image

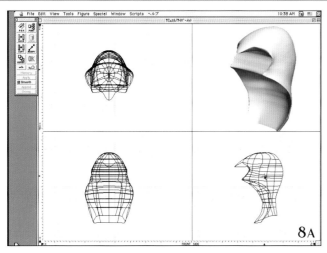

creating the helmet and headpiece

8A. The helmet was made by copying the form from the head and forming the 3D modeling shape around it.

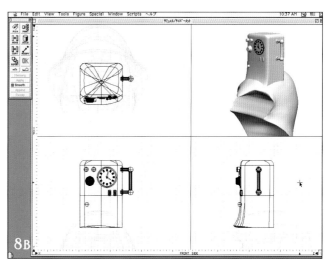

8B. For the speaker a rectangular extruded box was formed and fitted to the helmet.

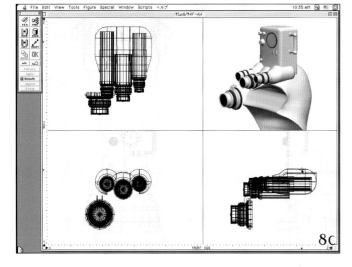

8C. A series of cylindrical tubes were made in various lengths, and their ends were fitted with smaller telescoping pieces.

8D. The trumpet was formed from one curved, modeled cylinder. **Tools›Memory›Sweep** was opened, and an open line was drawn through the center of the cylinder to form the trumpet flare shape. It was fit around the speaker. Details of the finished headpiece of instruments are shown below..

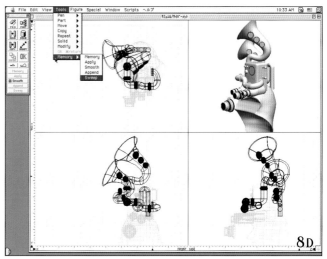

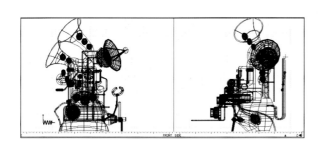

finishing the model

9A. An isometric view of the ray gun elements created in Shape.

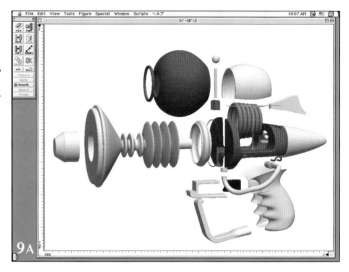

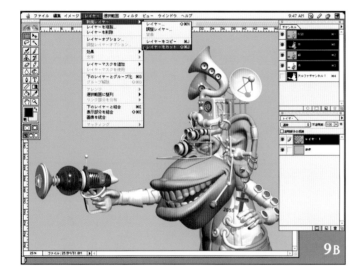

9B. A file of the completed model was opened in Adobe Photoshop. A new layer was created using **Layer›New›Layer**.

VirtualMedia A Step-By-Step Techniques Guide

final image

9C. A file was reproduced. Then, the image was reduced in size using **Image›Image Size,** and the setting was changed to Resolution: 72.

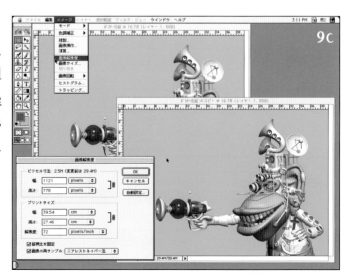

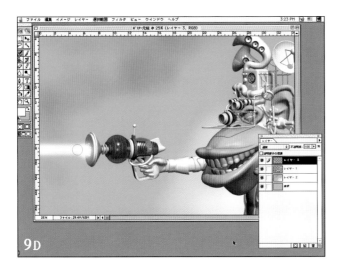

9D. The laser rays were painted using the Airbrush
Tool. Once the airbrushing was finished, the
resolution was changed back to its original setting.

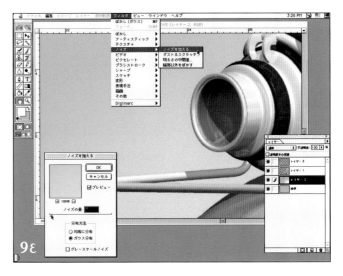

9ε. In Layer 1, **Filter›Noise›Add Noise**
was implemented.

f i n a l   i m a g e

GUITAR

PURPOSE advertising
DIGITAL CREATIVE yasutaka taga
CLIENT zeex tenjin
SOFTWARE shade and adobe photoshop

PAINTING

PURPOSE magazine cover
DIGITAL CREATIVE yasutaka taga
CLIENT ja-mar magazine
SOFTWARE shade and adobe photoshop

PIERCE

PURPOSE advertisement
DIGITAL CREATIVE yasutaka taga
CLIENT zeex tenjin
SOFTWARE shade and adobe photoshop

CYBER
ILLUSTRATION

Finally, technology is beginning to keep pace with artists'

visions. With a program like MetaCreations' Fractal Design

Painter, digital illustrators no longer have to settle for

an imitation palette: Software now provides a rich, infinite

toolbox of cyberbrushes, colors, textures and techniques for

LITTLE RED RIDING HOOD

PURPOSE promotional illustration
DIGITAL CREATIVE chet phillips
SOFTWARE painter 5.5

CHET PHILLIPS

There is perhaps no illustration technique as

exacting as scratchboard: The artist must carve

an image out of total blackness or whiteness.

Chet Phillips creates his cyber-scratchboard

working exclusively with MetaCreations Painter 5.5

to scratch and add color. The work has the flavor

creating the scratchboard technique

1A. A detailed pencil sketch was scanned into Adobe Photoshop and opened in MetaCreations Painter 5.5. **File›Clone** was selected to create a working copy of the drawing.

1A

1B

1B. The clone feature transformed the sketch into "tracing paper" which ghosted the image 50%. [⌘Command+F] opened the Fill dialog box, and the entire image was covered with black.

1C. The Pens medium was selected, and the Eraser Method was activated in the white Scratchboard Mode. This created clean, crisp areas of white in which to apply color.

final image

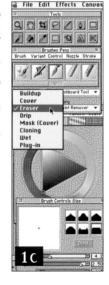

1C

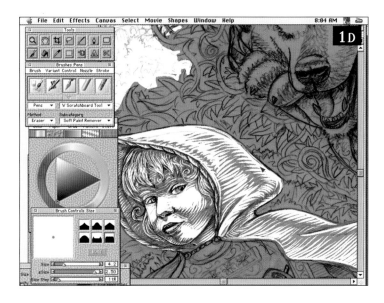

1 D. Using the Scratchboard Tool in the same manner as a traditional scratchboard pen. Areas of black were removed with a stroked texture from the girl's hood, hair and face.

1 E. [⌘Command+T] turned off the tracing paper. Specific white areas were reworked using the Scratchboard Tool, now configured to paint with black.

89

1 F. Numerous directional strokes representing the texture of the wolf's fur and the underbrush were added. Detail of the strokes are shown below.

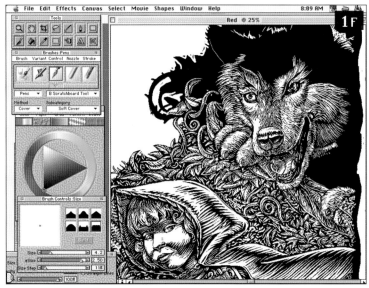

Using the Eraser Mode with the Scratchboard Tool does not leave any trace amount of white that might print as off-white.

virtual tips

1G. [⌘Command+T] turned on the tracing paper effect so that the progression of the illustration could be checked.

1H. With the black and white foreground completed, the border vine was created to frame the illustration.

1I. In the background, a grouping of trees intertwining with the border vine was added.

final image

creating the
color technique

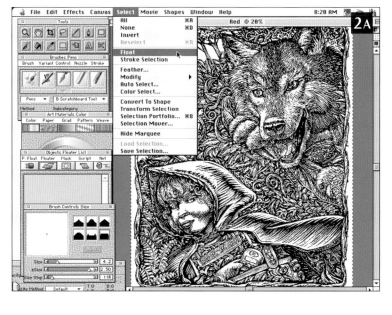

2A. Once the black and white scratchboard was complete, the entire image was selected with [⌘Command+A]. **Select›Float** was applied to initiate the coloring process.

2B. In the Controls palette, the floater attribute was changed from "Default" to "Gel". This made the white areas transparent and allowed color applied below to show through.

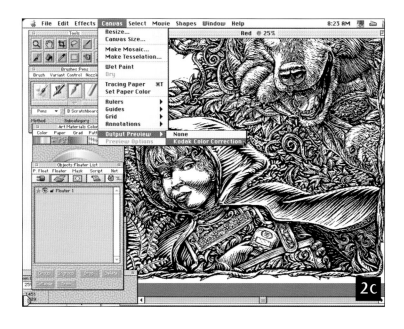

2C. **Canvas›Output Preview›Kodak Color Correction** was selected to restrict the color palette to more realistic CYMK values.

2D. In the Select Profiles dialog box, the Output Profile was set to: Photoshop RGB to CYMK.

2E. The Select Tool was utilized to mark the area of the underbrush. Using the Paint Bucket Tool, the selection was quickly covered with the green base color.

2F. To see how the illustration was progressing, the floater was turned off by clicking the eye icon in the Floater Palette.

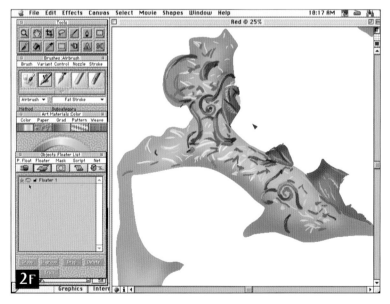

VirtualMedia A Step-By-Step Techniques Guide

final image

2G. Using the Airbrush and Scratchboard Tools, highlights and shadows in the scenery were painted with variations of browns and greens.

2H. Detail showing the colorized areas over the scratchboard technique.

2I. Brown areas of shadow color were applied to the wolf's coat. White sections were left open for highlight.

2J. Using the Airbrush Tool, tones of color were applied to the girl's face.

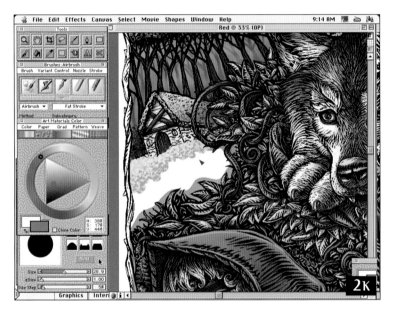

2K. To create depth within the forest, the tree trunks were airbrushed dark green.

2L. The floater was turned off to review the sections of color in progress.

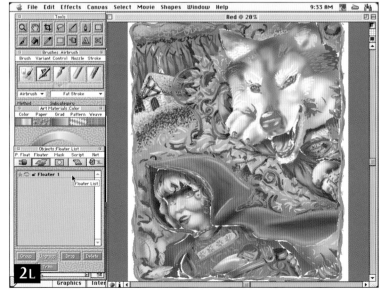

VirtualMedia A Step-By-Step Techniques Guide

final image

2M. A detail showing the wolf's tonal painting.

2N. The finished Illustration with final colors in place

final image

Bark Twain

PURPOSE one in a series of
literary animal illustrations

DIGITAL CREATIVE chet phillips

SOFTWARE painter 5.5

VirtualMedia

A Step-By-Step Techniques Guide

Cat Call

PURPOSE one from a series
"Cat's Got Your Tongue"

DIGITAL CREATIVE chet phillips

SOFTWARE painter 5.5

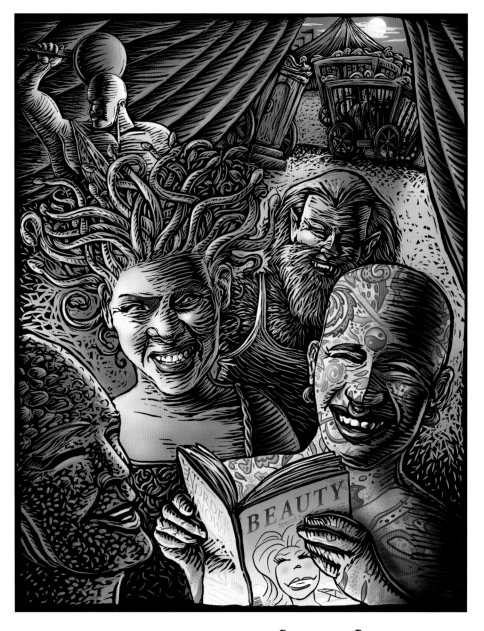

SKIN DEEP

PURPOSE promotional illustration

DIGITAL CREATIVE chet phillips

SOFTWARE painter 5.5

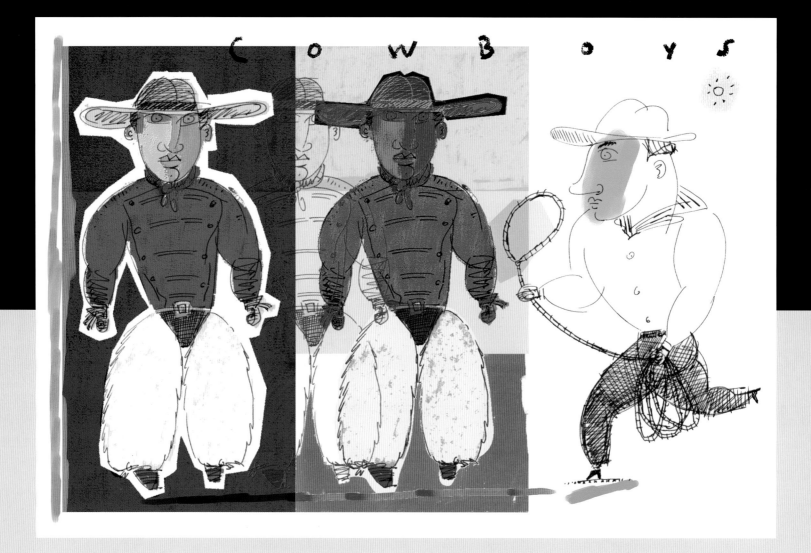

COWBOYS

PURPOSE promotional illustration
DIGITAL CREATIVE susan le van
CLIENT le van/barbee studio
SOFTWARE metacreations fractal painter

susan
LeVan

Susan LeVan keeps her imagery intuitive, exploratory

and playful because she wants her cyber illustration

work to be accessible. Often, the figures are basic

structures that she builds upon with color, texture

and even incidental marks. LeVan uses MetaCreations

Fractal Painter and a Wacom tablet, but believes

her draw-then-color technique provides the same

aesthetic as traditional illustration. Using modified

brushes and building layer upon layer, LeVan creates

what she terms the frozen moment: A single frame

implies an entire world beyond, she says.

creating the line art

A. Ball point pen drawings of cowboys "A" and "B" were scanned into Adobe Photoshop in black and white at 150dpi. Next they were brought into MetaCreations Painter 5.5. Using the Magic Wand and Delete, the gray tones were cleaned.

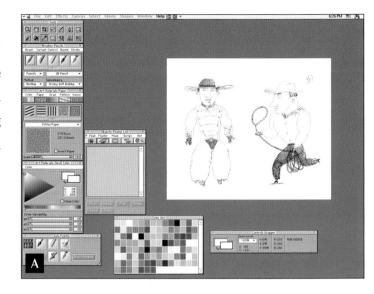

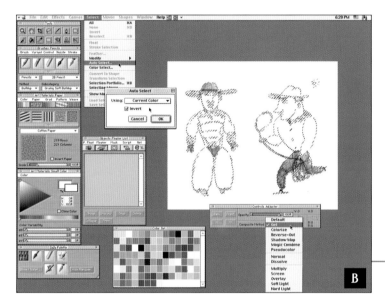

B. The white background color was chosen with the Eyedropper Tool. **Select›Auto Select** was opened, the Invert setting was checked while the Current Color was chosen. The selection was floated using the Pointing Finger Icon on the Tools Palette. To soften and darken the lines, Composite Method: Gel was chosen in the Controls: Adjuster Palette.

creating cowboy #1

1A. A new file of cowboy "A" was opened. [⌘Command+C] copied and [⌘Command+V] pasted the image, leaving it as a floater. [⌘Command+A] selected the area, and [⌘Command+F] opened the Fill dialog box. The background canvas was filled with pale yellow by checking Fill With: Current Color.

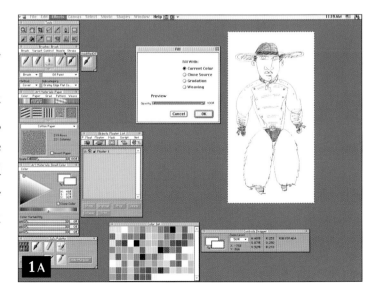

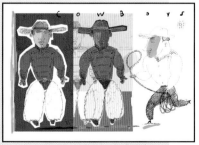

final image

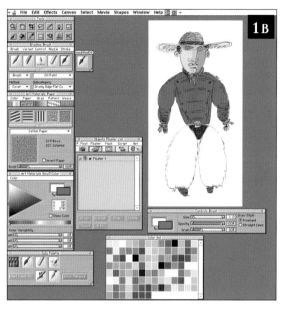

1B. In the Controls Brush dialog box the Size was set to 1.0. In the Color Variability Palette, the HSV settings were adjusted to 0%. The background canvas was then painted using the Modified Oil Brush.

1C. The hat was chosen using the Shape Design Tool. From the Objects Floaters List, the copy was floated. In the Controls: Adjuster Palette, Composite Method: Reverse Out was selected. The gloves and pants were chosen with the Shape Design Tool. In the Controls: Adjuster Palette, Composite Method: Colorize was selected. The floaters were merged with the background canvas by clicking Drop from the Floaters List.

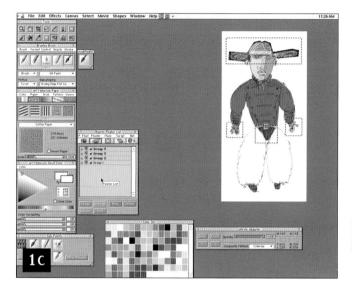

1D. [⌘Command+A] selected the area and **Select›Float** created the floater. [⌘Command+F] opened the Fill dialog box, and the background canvas was filled with red as the Current Color. In the Controls: Adjuster Palette, Composite Method: Colorize was selected.

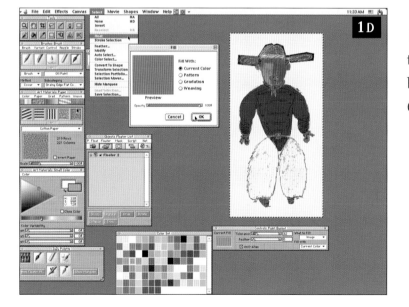

1E. Using the Shape Design Tool, the lower part of the body was outlined in purple.

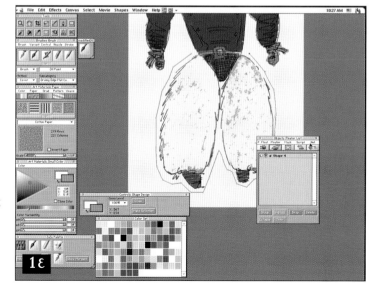

1F. After connecting the outline, it was filled in as a solid and was automatically named Shape 4 in the Floaters Palette. The Group button was clicked to rasterize the image.

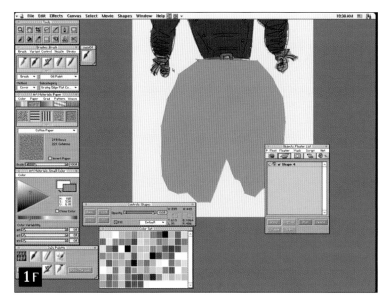

1G. In the Controls Adjuster Palette, Composite Method: Colorize was selected to colorize the chaps. The Magic Wand was used to select the pink area and mask it off.

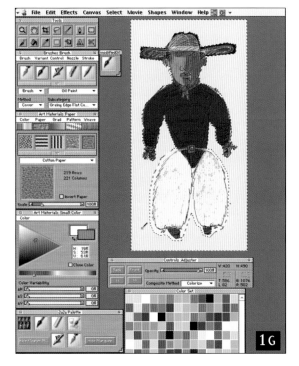

1H. To make the lower box, the Scratchboard Tool Brush with pale yellow was used. Using the Paintbucket Tool, the outside pink area was filled with pale yellow.

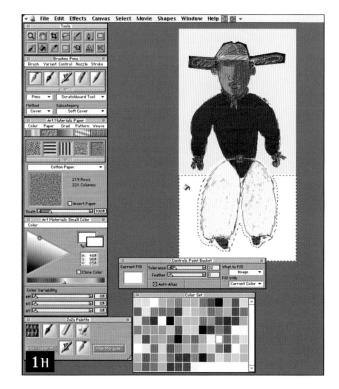

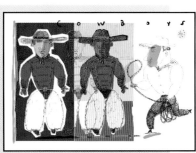

final image

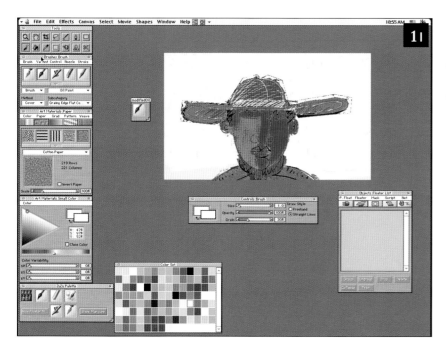

1 I. The area around the head was painted with pale yellow using the Modified Oil Brush Tool.

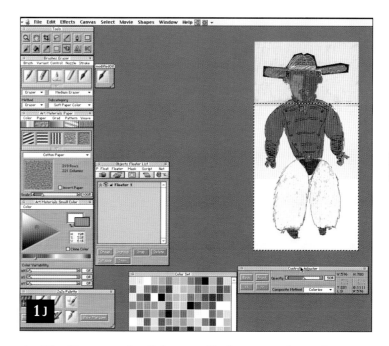

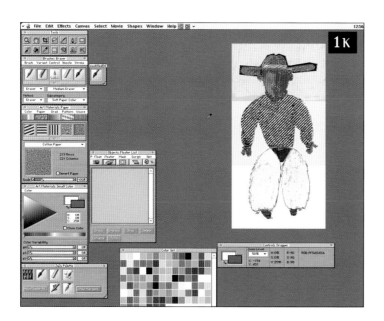

1 J. The Rectangular Selection Tool was used to select the lower two-thirds of the image. In the Controls: Adjuster Palette, Composite Method: Colorize and Opacity: 50% were selected. In the Objects Floater List, Drop was clicked.

1 K. Using the Eyedropper Tool, the shirt color was selected and painted dark gray with the Modified Oil Brush. The file was then saved as Cowboy #1.

Using MetaCreations Painter 5.5 gives the artist an infinite combination of brushes with wet or dry mediums.

virtual tips

creating cowboy #2

2A. To begin cowboy #2, [⌘Command+A] selected the image from Cowboy #1 and **Effects›Tonal Control›Negative** was activated.

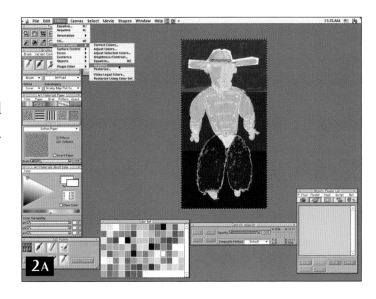

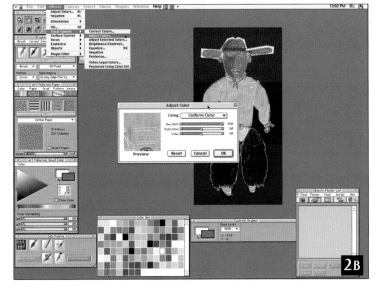

2B. **Effects›Tonal Control›Adjust Color** was opened. In the Adjust Color dialog box, Uniform Color was chosen and the Hue slider was moved all the way to +50%.

2C. The upper third of Cowboy #1 was floated using the Rectangular Selection Tool. It was pasted onto Cowboy #2 using [⌘Command+V]. In the Controls: Adjuster Palette, Composite Method: Colorize was chosen. The file was saved as Cowboy #2.

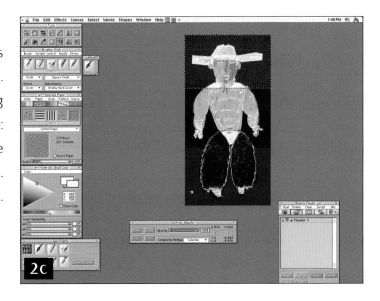

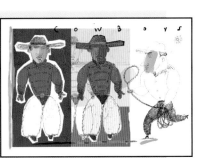

final image

VirtualMedia A Step-By-Step Techniques Guide

finalizing the cowboys

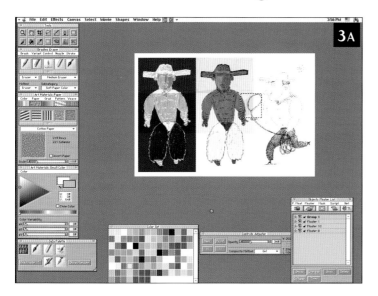

3A. [⌘Command+A] selected and [⌘Command+C] copied Cowboys #1 and #2. They were pasted into a larger horizontal file using [⌘Command+V]. Cowboy "B" was retrieved and placed onto the large image. Composite Method: Gel was selected. A yellow shape was created with the Shape Design Tool and pasted as a Composite Method: Gel.

3B. Using the Square Chalk in the Brushes Palette, a yellow patch for the sun was made as a separate file. **Select›Auto Select** was opened. The Current Color was used while the Invert Box was checked.

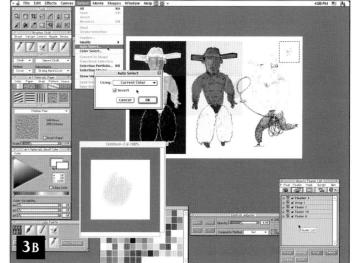

105

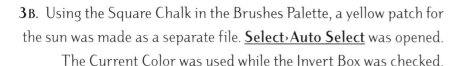

3C. The line drawing of Cowboy "A" was pasted into the image. In the Controls: Adjuster Palette, Composite Method: Gel was selected and filled with red.

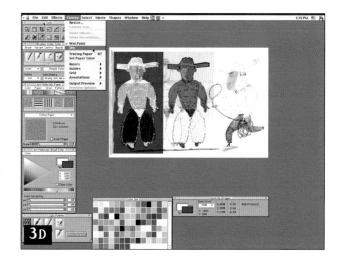

3D. Dark green was applied to the cowboy panel on the left with the Square Chalk Brush. Using the Simple Water Color Brush, the right cowboy's face and feet were painted blue. **Canvas›Dry** was applied from the drop down menu.

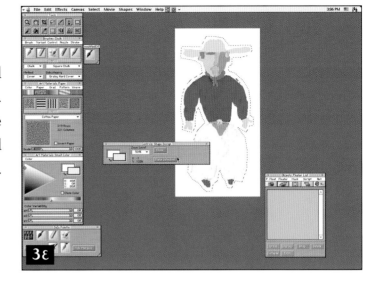

3ε. At this point, the illustration was re-evaluated and revised. The first version of Cowboy #1 was reopened. Using the Shape Design Tool, a crude cut-out of the painted figure was outlined. The shape was closed and Make Selection was chosen in the Controls Palette.

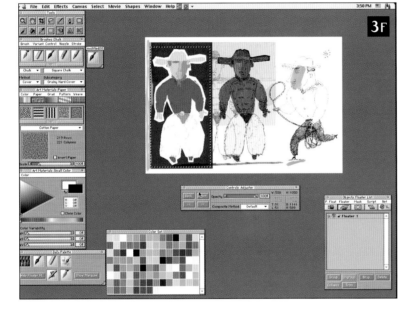

3ғ. [⌘Command+C] copied and [⌘Command+V] pasted the selection into the larger file. In the Controls: Adjuster Palette, Composite Method: Default was chosen.

3ɢ. A black line version of Cowboy "A" was pasted over the newly placed figure.

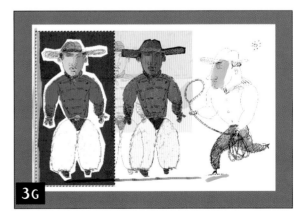

final image

VirtualMedia A Step-By-Step Techniques Guide

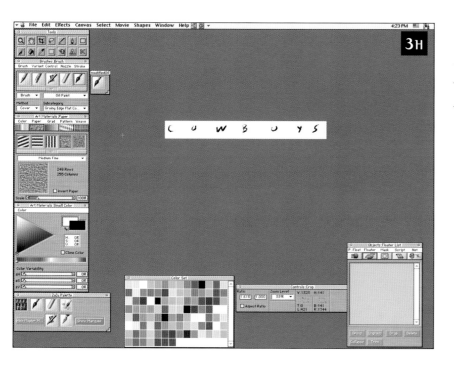

3H. The word "cowboys" was painted in black as a separate file using the Modified Oil Brush. It was pasted into the larger file composited as a Gel.

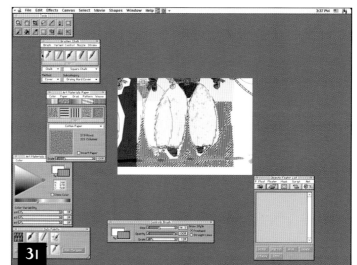

107

3I. Using orange Square Chalk on Cotton Paper, the ground area of the center figure was colored to complete the illustration.

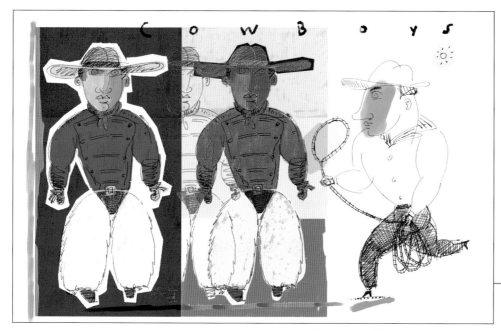

final image

WALKING THE SHOW DOG

PURPOSE promotional illustration
DIGITAL CREATIVE susan le van
& ernest barbee
CLIENT le van/barbee studio
SOFTWARE metacreations fractal painter

VirtualMedia

MONKEY TAUNTS

PURPOSE promotional illustration
DIGITAL CREATIVE susan le van
CLIENT le van/barbee studio
SOFTWARE metacreations fractal painter

RIDING ON THE RANGE

PURPOSE promotional illustration
DIGITAL CREATIVE susan le van
CLIENT le van/barbee studio
SOFTWARE metacreations fractal painter

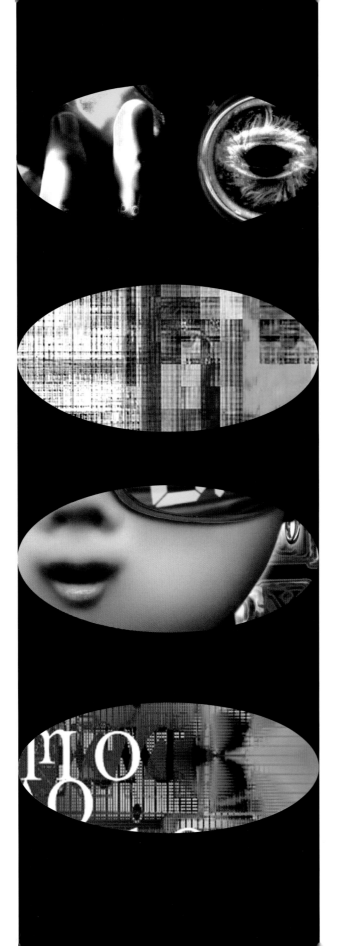

FILTERS
AND EFFECTS

An infinite medley of tools and techniques is what creates

the magic in art created with filters and special effects.

Using Adobe Photoshop with plug-in software such as Andrews

Filters, Cheap Video Tricks and Kai's Power Tools, artists can

blend, blur, filter and merge effect upon effect until the

desired level of mystery is reached. John and David Jenson

of Designaholix customize their visions with lighting,

blurring and over-saturation, while Gustavo Machado applies

filter after filter to explode his imagery into a new, found

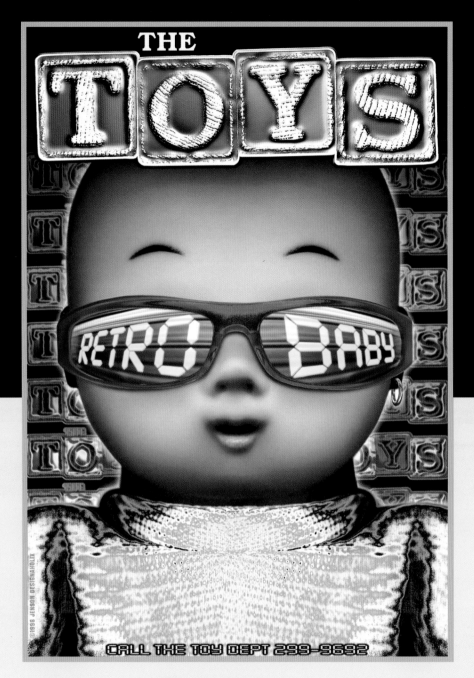

The Toys

PURPOSE promotional poster for the band "the toys"
DIGITAL CREATIVE jenson designaholix
CLIENT the toys
SOFTWARE adobe photoshop

Jenson
DesignaHolix

John and David Jenson are two very different

brothers who share the same objectives: to stretch

the limits of design through extreme creativity and

technological mastery. John trained as an artist;

David as an engineer. Today, using a flatbed

scanner as a digital camera, Adobe Photoshop and

their computers as a digital darkroom, they unite

many planes of imagery into windows of fantastic

impossibilities. The Jensons are always looking

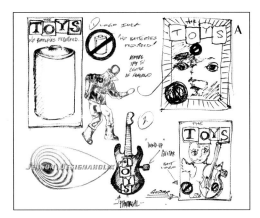

sketches

A. A rock band asked Jenson Designaholix to design its poster. After seeing the band live, Jenson Designaholix developed intriguing initial concepts.

B. Rough drafts were developed in the computer.

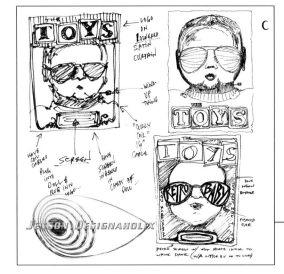

C. Finalized layouts were then prepared indicating the placement of the elements.

creating the toys logo

final image

1A. Toy blocks were scanned into Adobe Photoshop. **<u>Select›Color Range</u>** was used to select the dark shaded areas of the blocks. The selection was saved as a channel.

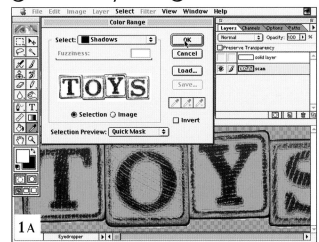

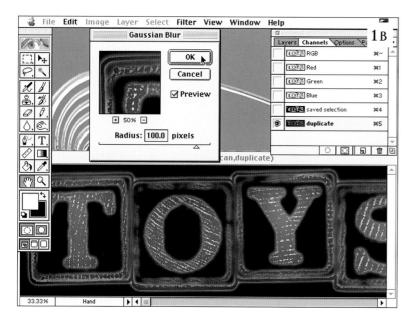

1B. In the Channels Palette, a duplicate was made. **Filter›Gaussian Blur** was used to blur the duplicate channel. The original "saved selection" was loaded and **Filter›Gaussian Blur** was used a second time.

Note: A portion of the Jenson Designaholix screen logo is visible in the background.

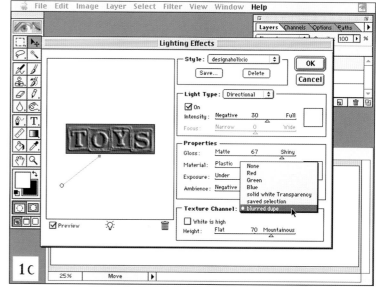

1C. A new layer named "solid white" was created. **Filter›Render›Lighting Effects** was opened. In the Texture Channel box, Blurred Dupe was selected.

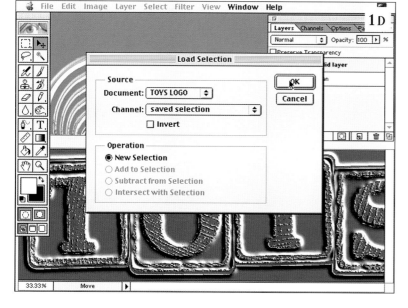

1D. A new layer was created with **Layer›New›Layer** and named "Frosting." Using **Select›Load Selection** the "saved selection" was reloaded.

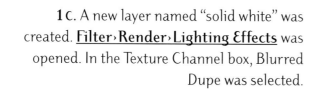

*To apply a clean cut-out from behind an object, select the background with the Lasso Tool, and choose **Edit>Clear**.*

virtual tips

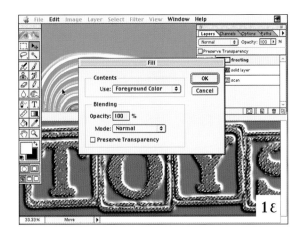

1ε. Using **Edit›Fill**, the toy blocks image was filled with the foreground color.

1F. The Lasso Tool was used to select around the blocks. **Edit›Clear** was then used to remove pixels from the perimeter of each block.

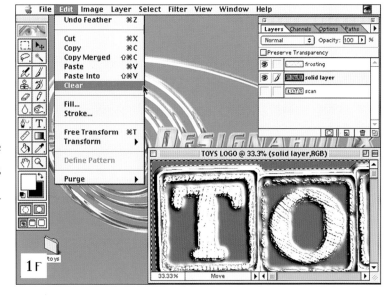

VirtualMedia A Step-By-Step Techniques Guide

1G. On the "solid layer," a selection was made around one of the blocks with the Lasso Tool. Using [⌘Command+U] the Hue/Saturation dialog box was opened, and the colorize box was checked. The hue, saturation and lightness were adjusted to produce vivid colors. This procedure was repeated with each remaining block.

creating the doll image

final image

2A. A doll was placed on the flatbed and scanned into Adobe Photoshop. When three dimensional objects are scanned on the flatbed, dust can appear and cause defects. The Rubber Stamp Tool was used to remove the blemishes.

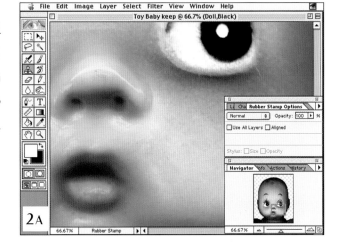

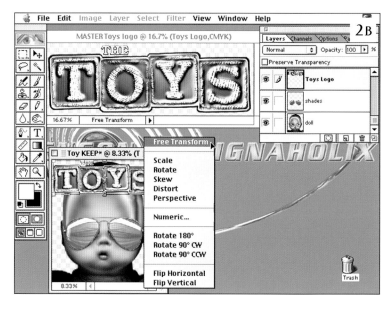

2B. Sunglasses were scanned on the flatbed and placed into Adobe Photoshop. The same clean up procedure was used to remove all defects.

2C. As the project progressed, a different pair of sunglasses were scanned. The client requested that the doll project a positive facial expression. Through digital editing, eyebrows were added and with the Smudge Tool, the mouth was changed to a smile.

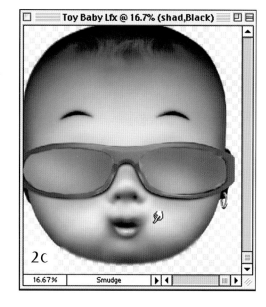

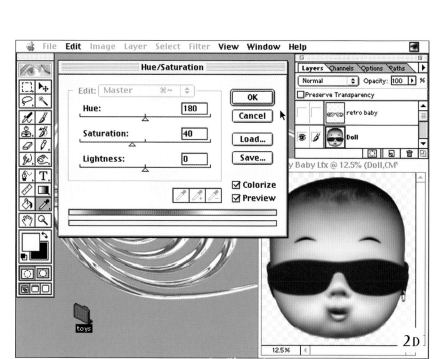

2D. In this step, [⌘Command+U] opened the Hue/Saturation dialog box. The doll was colorized in blue by adjusting the Saturation slider, to portray the doll as a toy and not a real baby.

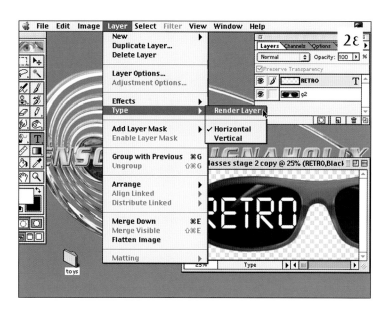

2ε. With the previously scanned sunglasses, **Layer › Type › Render Layer** was applied to create the words, "Retro Baby."

2F. [⌘Control+Click+Hold] opened the Contextural Menu. The text was then altered in perspective.

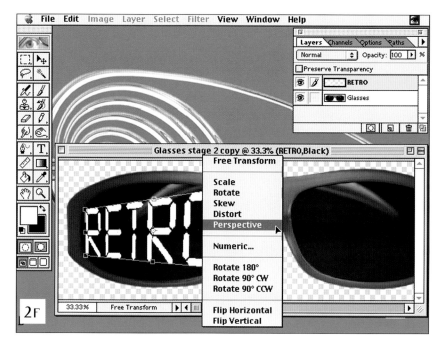

THE
TOYS
RETRO BABY

final image

2G. A duplicate of the layer named "Retro Baby" was made. A gaussian blur was applied to the bottom layer with a Radius of 10 pixels and named Retro Baby Blur. The glowing neon effect was created by combining two layers Retro Baby and Retro Baby Blur. The underlying layer was blurred and the top remained sharp.

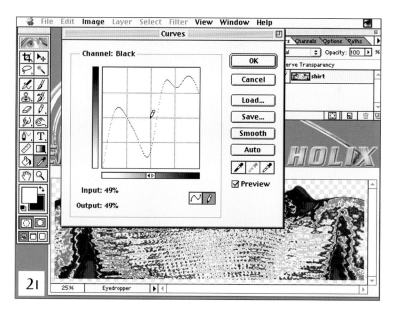

2H. To colorize the glasses and type, [⌘Command+U] opened the Hue/Saturation dialog box, and settings were adjusted to obtain the appropriate color.

119

2I. The doll's sweater was scanned and opened in Adobe Photoshop. Using [⌘Command+M], the Curves dialog box was opened and the setting was altered to give the sweater a metallic effect.

final image

Moloko CD Tray Card

PURPOSE cd tray card
DIGITAL CREATIVES jenson designaholix, holly messer
CLIENT moloko shivers
SOFTWARE adobe photoshop

VirtualMedia

Eyez Heard a Shot

PURPOSE image from promotional cd
DIGITAL CREATIVE jenson designaholix
CLIENT designaholix
SOFTWARE adobe photoshop

Art With a Bite

PURPOSE promotional postcard
DIGITAL CREATIVE jenson designaholix, holly messer
CLIENT designaholix
SOFTWARE adobe photoshop

RUMO
AO
SÉCULO
XXI

gustavo machado

<u>GOING THROUGH THE 21st CENTURY</u>

<u>PURPOSE</u> digital wallpaper
<u>DIGITAL CREATIVE</u> gustavo machado
<u>CLIENT</u> gustavo machado design
<u>SOFTWARE</u> adobe photoshop

Gustavo Machado

Gustavo Machado's electronic toolbox is as large

as his organic images are deep. Adobe Photoshop,

KPT 3, KPT Convolver, Xaos Tools, AlienSkin Black

Box, Andromeda Series, AutoF/X, DigiEffects,

Extensis Photo Text, Filter Factory, Andrew Filters,

MetaCreations Painter and CorelDraw are among

his favorite tools. He first scans found objects and

photos, then passes them through filter after filter

until the images appear to be in flux: morphing

from the past to the present or vice versa.

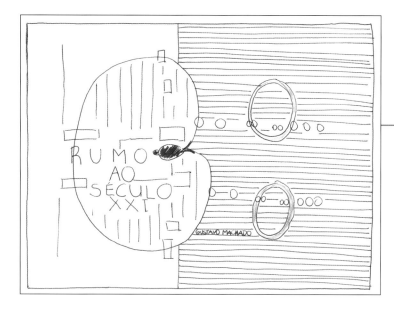

sketch

Sketch. A rough concept layout was drawn indicating the elements of the design.

creating the background layer

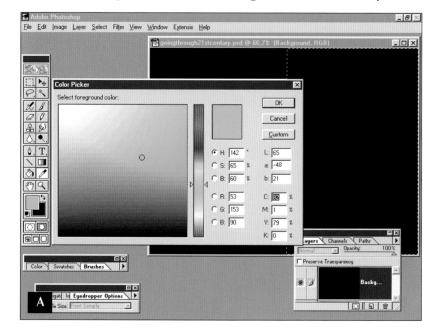

A. A new RGB file was created, 800 x 600 pixels with a black background color. The Color Picker dialog box was selected and a new foreground RGB green color was defined: R 53, G 153, B 90. Using the rectangular Marquee Tool, image half was selected 400 x 600 pixels.

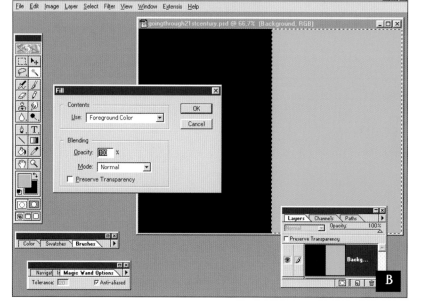

B. Using the rectangular Marquee Tool, half of the image was selected 400 x 600 pixels. **Edit›Fill** was used to fill the selection with the new green foreground color.

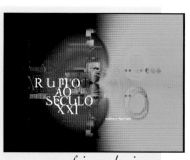

final image

C. To create a border fade, the Gradient Tool was used on the left portion of the selection. The Gradient Editor dialog box was set to Foreground to Transparent.

creating layer 1

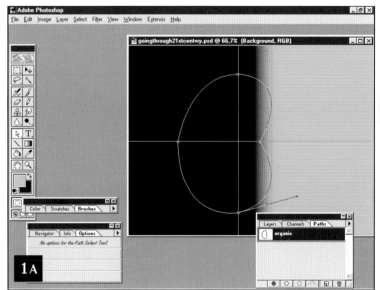

1A. An organic shape was created with the Pen Tool and then saved as "organic."

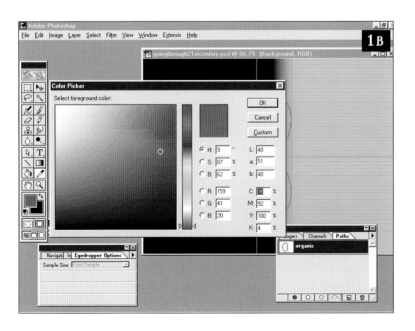

1B. The Color Picker dialog box was selected and a new foreground RGB red color was defined: R 159, G 41, B 20.

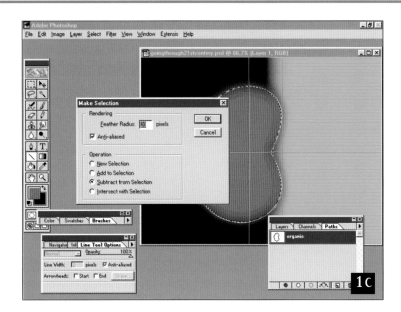

1C. From the Paths window, the Make Selection dialog box was opened. The setting was adjusted to Feather Radius: 20 pixels. The red fill was then applied.

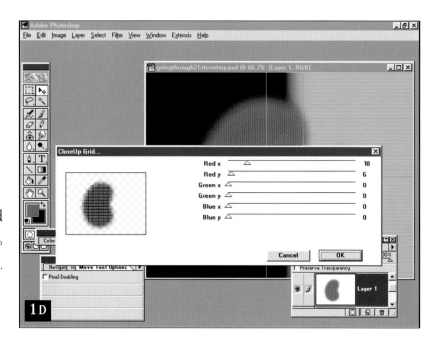

1D. To create a soft grid texture, CloseUp Grid filter was applied to the selection with 50% Opacity and Soft Light Mode.

VirtualMedia A Step-By-Step Techniques Guide

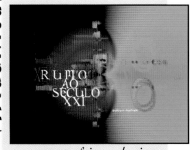

final image

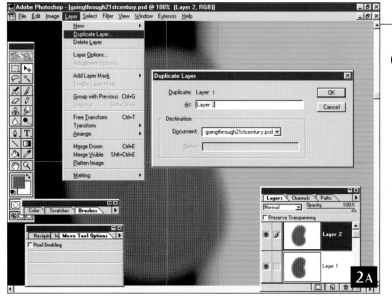

creating layer 2

2A. To create Layer 2, Layer 1 was duplicated, using the **Layer›Duplicate Layer**.

2B. Layer 2 was dragged to the right below Layer 1. Using [⌘Command+U] the Hue/Saturation dialog box was opened. To enhance the color, the settings were changed to Hue: -126, Saturation: +31 and Lightness: -15.

creating layer 3

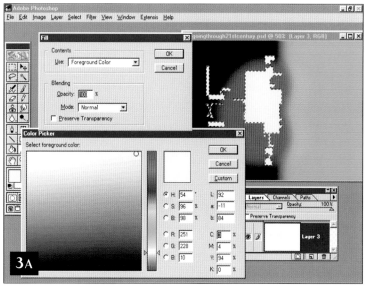

127

3A. A new layer was created by clicking the layer icon in the Layers window. With the Path and Marquee Tools, geometric forms were drawn over the organic shape. The Color Picker dialog box was selected and a new foreground yellow color was defined: R: 251, G: 228, B: 10. [⌘Command+F] was used to fill the selection.

3B. Cheap Video Trick was used on the selection to apply a checked pattern similar to microchips.

❧ Using the CloseUp Grid and Cheap Video Trick filters allow for a diverse range of textural effects.

virtual tips

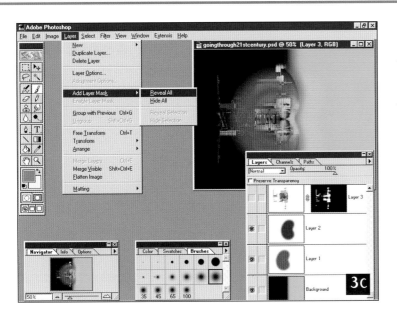

3C. **Layer›Add Layer Mask›Reveal All** was applied to Layer 3. Erase and Airbrush Tools were used to add detail to the composition.

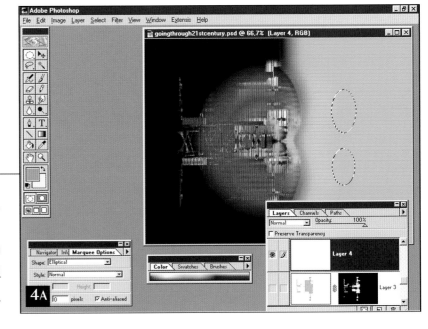

creating layer 4

4A. A new layer was created by clicking the layer icon in the Layers Palette. Two ellipses were then created with the elliptical Marquee Tool.

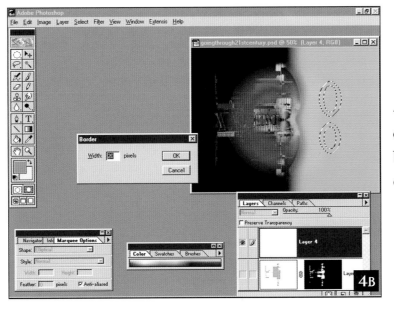

4B. **Select›Modify Border** opened the Border dialog box. The setting was changed to Width: 20.

final image

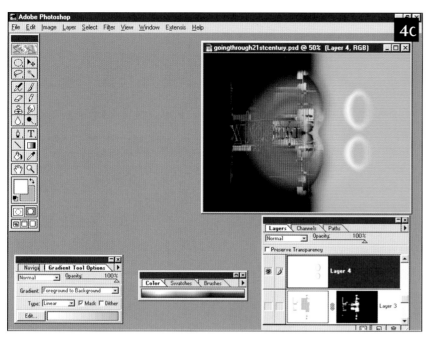

4C. With the Gradient Tool, the selections were filled with a yellow-to-green gradation.

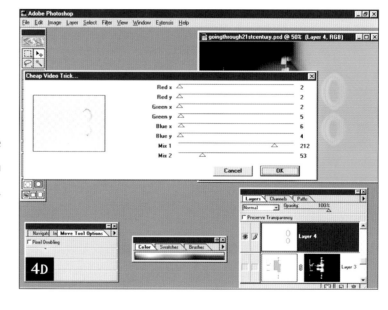

4D. Cheap Video Trick was used on the selection to apply a video pattern similar to TV lines.

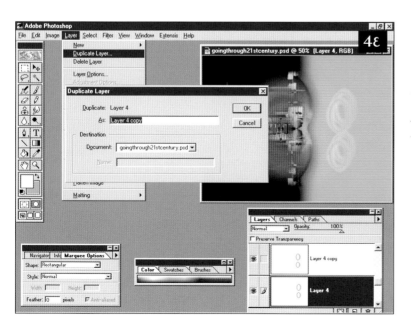

4E. The rings were reproduced using **Layer>Duplicate Layer** and then shifted to the bottom left.

creating layer 5

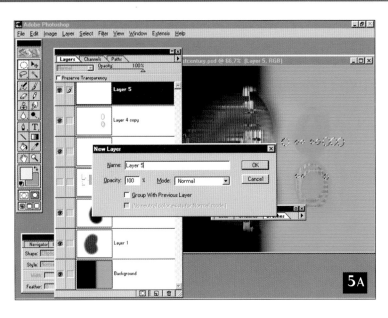

5A. Layer 5 was made by clicking the layers icon in the Layers palette. Several circles were created using the elliptical Marquee Tool.

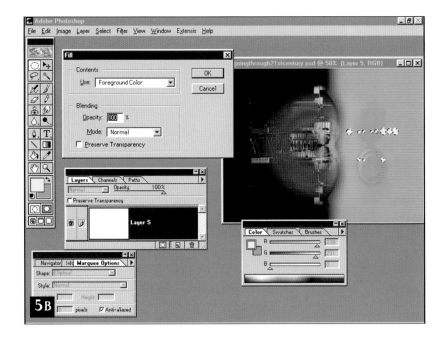

5B. [⌘Command+F] opened the Fill dialog box. The selected circles were filled with the yellow foreground color.

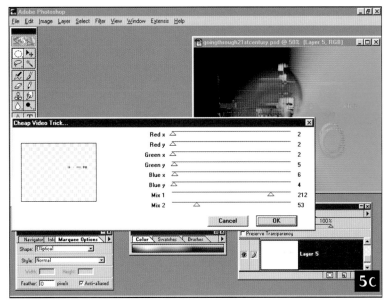

5C. Cheap Video Trick was used on the selection to apply a checked pattern similar to microchips.

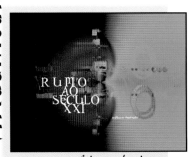

final image

creating layer 6

6A. Layer 6 was made by clicking the layers icon in the Layers Palette. The Type Tool dialog box was opened and "Rumo Ao Seculo XXI" (Going through the 21st century) was typed using the Confusebox font at 55pts.

creating layer 7

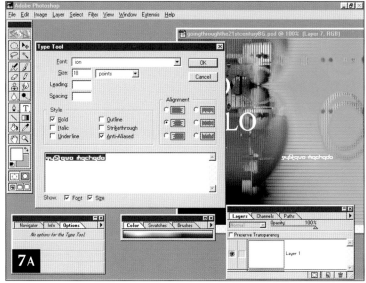

7A. The Type Tool dialog box was opened, and the artist's name was inserted using the Icon font at 18 points.

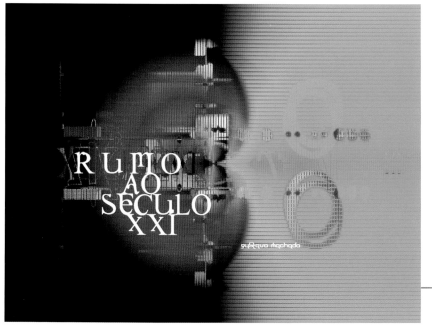

f i n a l   i m a g e

ANTI-MATERIA

PURPOSE website
DIGITAL CREATIVE gustavo machado
CLIENT anti-materia
SOFTWARE adobe photoshop

VirtualMedia

CURSO DE WEB DESIGN

PURPOSE website
DIGITAL CREATIVE gustavo machado
CLIENT ENG DTP & multimedia
SOFTWARE adobe photoshop

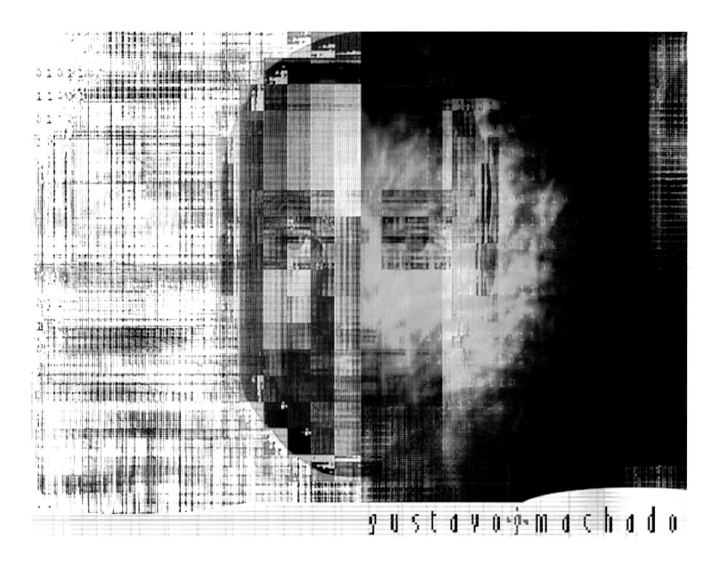

gustavo machado

WIRED

PURPOSE promotional interface
DIGITAL CREATIVE gustavo machado
CLIENT gustavo machado design
SOFTWARE adobe photoshop

TYPOGRAPHY

Raising type from the one-dimensional plane into three-dimensional

space is the goal of these featured artists. Software such as

Adobe Dimensions and Adobe Illustrator can float letterforms in

space, as they do in Tom White's work. His elegantly rendered

cyber-illuminations contain many highlights, shadows, and beveled

edges, which trick the eye into accepting their apparent realism.

Rafael Peixoto Ferreira communicates through vernacular references

of life intertwined with type. Both artists reveal the art of the

letterform, using high technology to bring new appreciation to one

10 Top Companies to Work For

PURPOSE editorial special section cover
DIGITAL CREATIVE tom white
CLIENT interactive week
SOFTWARE adobe dimensions, illustrator & photoshop

TOM WHITE

Tom White's artistic world is solidly built on

dimensional type. Shapes and letterforms connect and

mesh, forming intricate structures with undeniable

style. In fact, one of his most meaningful inspirations

is architecture. Concept is most important to White.

He pulls from both his illustration and design skills

to find a solution that reinforces the concept.

Importing and exporting numerous times between

Adobe Illustrator and Adobe Photoshop, the artist

creating the letterforms

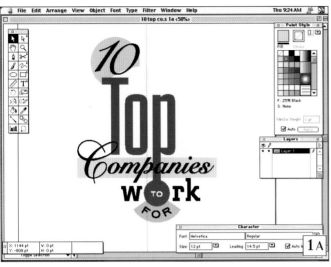

1A. In Adobe Illustrator, working fonts were chosen, and a rough layout of the type elements was constructed. Once the design was finalized, the elements were saved as art files.

1B. Curved, dashed lines were included accenting the shape of the type. A wavy swirl was made to indicate steam from a coffee cup that would be added later.

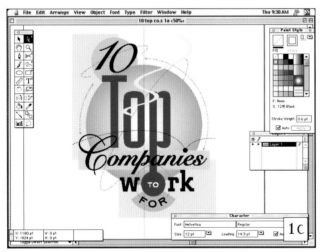

1C. Additional shaded background areas were included in the design. Elements were positioned in these areas later.

final image

1D. Elements of the type designs were then brought into Adobe Dimensions from Adobe Illustrator to add shape and dimension to the letterforms. The direction of the lighting was determined by clicking the sphere in the Lighting window. In the Surface Properties window Ambient was adjusted to 20%.

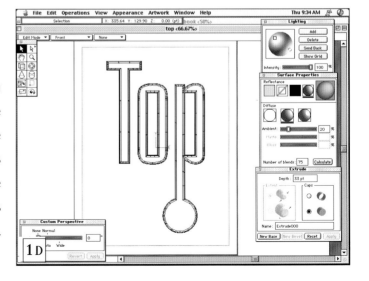

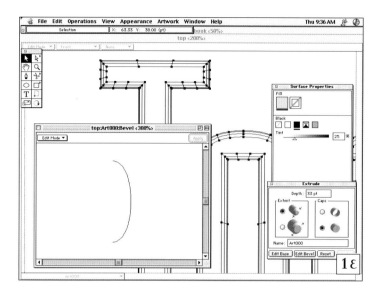

1ε. The art file of the word "top" was given a rounded bevel. In the Extrude window, the setting was adjusted to Depth: 33pt.

1F. The Adobe Illustrator art file "companies" was imported into Adobe Dimensions. The Tint was set to 25%.

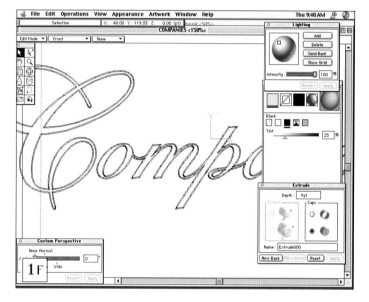

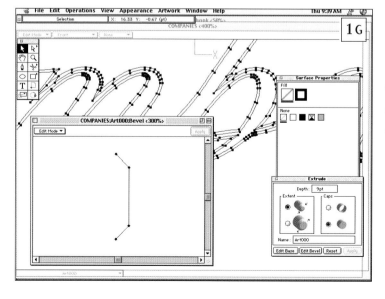

1G. "Companies" was given a sharp angular bevel. In the Extrude window, the setting was adjusted to Depth: 9pt.

In Adobe Dimensions, the extruded bevel window option allows for a variety of rounded or angled bevels, in various sizes, to be applied to the type.

virtual tips

creating the building

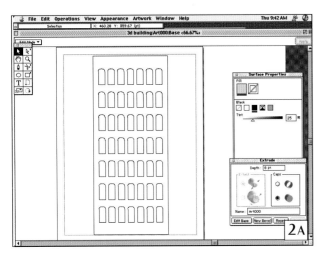

2A. A simple line drawing of a building façade, created in Adobe Illustrator, was imported into Adobe Dimensions.

2B. The façade was duplicated and rotated to the side of the original façade to form a building with dimension. In the Custom Perspective window, the Angle slider was used to adjust the perspective of the building. In the Lighting window, the light direction was made to match the letterforms.

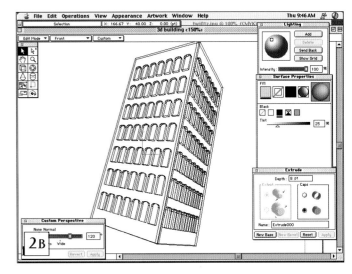

2C. The building structure was opened in Adobe Photoshop. With the Gradient Tool, shadows and soft lighting were applied to the overall surface. A stone texture was applied to the surface using a soft light value of 15%, to keep the image subtle.

creating the circular window

3A. A beveled circle for the circular window was drawn in Adobe Illustrator that would be added later.

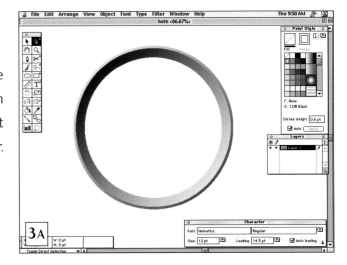

VirtualMedia A Step-By-Step Techniques Guide

final image

creating shade and highlight to the type

4A. All the type elements were imported into Adobe Photoshop and pasted into position in layers. Shading and subtle highlights were added to give additional dimension to the letterforms.

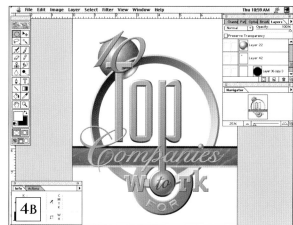

4B. The circular window was added and placed behind the type layout. A horizontal band was positioned behind "companies" to enhance the readability of the type.

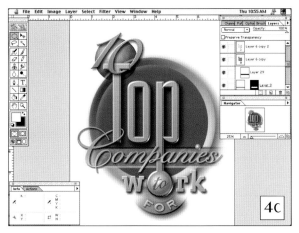

4C. Shadows were included to lift the elements and create more texture and dimension.

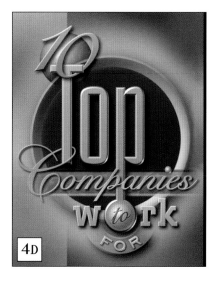

4D. Background sections with shading were added to emphasize the central area of type.

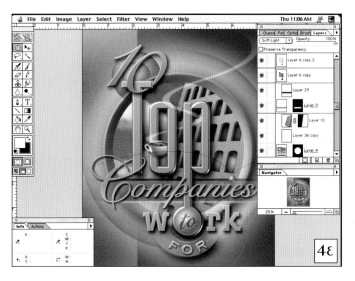

4ε. The building was positioned behind the circular window. An existing image of a coffee cup was placed in the layout under the white swirl of steam.

creating the color

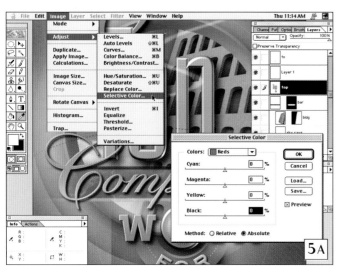

5A. The file was converted to RGB. Using **Image › Adjust › Selective Color**, and each element was given color in the white, neutral and black density.

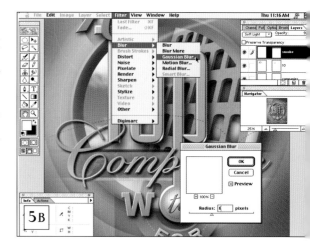

5B. Using **Filter › Gaussian Blur**, the steam trail from the coffee cup was blurred.

5C. The image was then flattened using Flatten Image from the Layers palette.

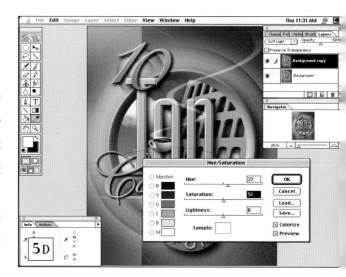

5D. In the Layers window, the image floated above itself. The layer was set to softlight and Opacity 50%, to add a slight boost to the color and contrast. Using [⌘Command+U] the Hue/Saturation dialog box was opened and the settings were adjusted slightly to add subtle color.

final image

VirtualMedia A Step-By-Step Techniques Guide

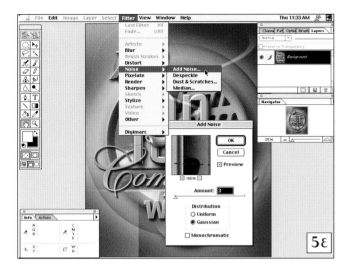

5ε. The image was flattened again.
Filter›Noise›Add Noise was opened
and the setting was adjusted to Amount: 3.

5F. **Image›Mode›CMYK Color** was used to change the color mode.

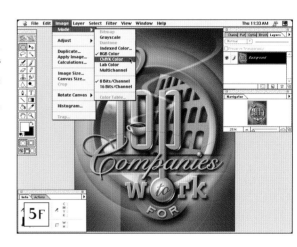

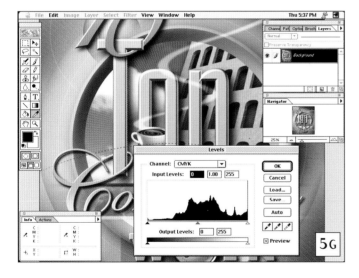

5G. **Image›Adjust›Levels** was opened, and slight color adjustments were made to the overall image.

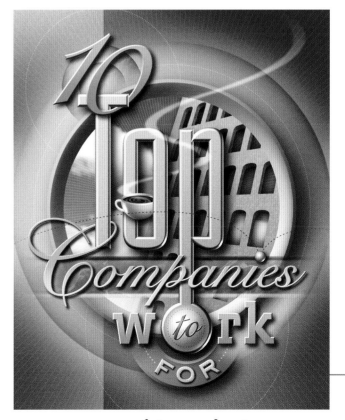

f i n a l   i m a g e

A Step-By-Step Techniques Guide

VirtualMedia

OFFICE 2000
VISUAL GUIDE

PURPOSE editorial feature spread
DIGITAL CREATIVE tom white
CLIENT windows magazine
SOFTWARE adobe dimensions, illustrator & photoshop

GUIDE TO
INTERNET EXPLORER 5

PURPOSE editorial feature
DIGITAL CREATIVE tom white
CLIENT windows magazine
SOFTWARE adobe dimensions,
illustrator & photoshop

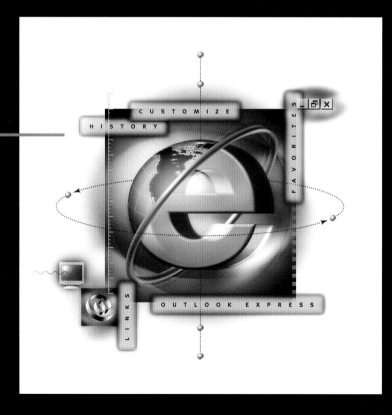

Voice Over the Internet

PURPOSE editorial cover

DIGITAL CREATIVE tom white

CLIENT netware connections magazine

SOFTWARE adobe dimensions, illustrator & photoshop

VIDEO CHAOS

PURPOSE promotion
DIGITAL CREATIVE rafael ferreira
CLIENT rafa ferreira design
SOFTWARE adobe photoshop & pixar typestry

RaFael PeixoTo Ferreira

When solving a communication problem for a

client, Rafael Peixoto Ferreira looks for what he

calls "corporate subcultures". He works to reveal

alternate meanings in everyday concepts and

objects. In conveying these new interpretations,

the artist wants to elicit a genuine, emotional

reaction from his audience. Mixing 3D type,

photos, and elements from retro illustrations with

Photoshop, Pixar Typestry, Painter and CorelDraw,

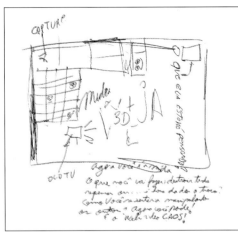

sketch

Sketch. A sketch was developed to illustrate video conferencing around the world.

creating the video images

1A. Screen captures from the web were imported into Adobe Photoshop. Using the Marquee Tool, selected images were inverted using **Image›Adjust›Invert**.

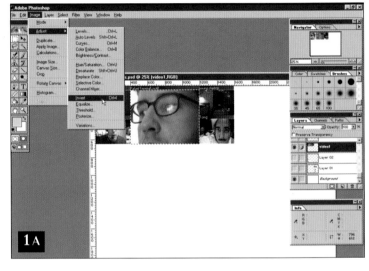

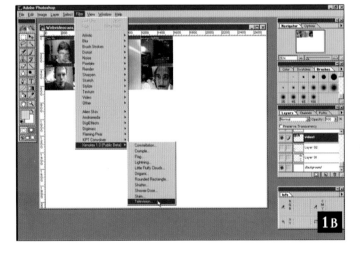

1B. **Filters›Xenofex›Television** was opened to create a low-resolution television screen line effect.

1C. In the Xenofex Television dialog box, settings were adjusted to Scanline Strength: 34 and Scanline Thickness: 4. All the screen captures were placed on different layers in the composition.

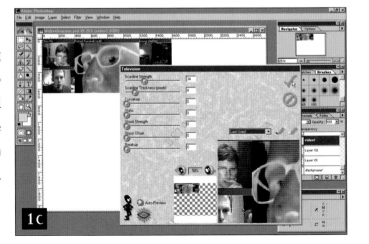

final image

VirtualMedia A Step-By-Step Techniques Guide

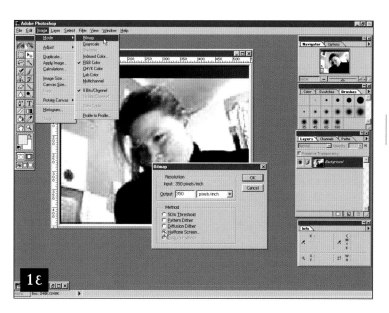

1D. A photo of a woman was imported into Adobe Photoshop. **Image›Mode›Grayscale** was applied to the color image.

149

1Ɛ. Using **Image›Mode›Bitmap**, the photo was then converted to a bitmapped image. In the Bitmap dialog box, the settings were adjusted to Output: 350 pixels/inch and Method: Halftone Screen.

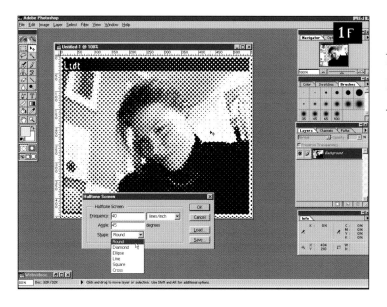

1F. In the Halftone Screen dialog box, the settings were adjusted to Frequency: 40 lines/inch, Angle: 45 and Shape: Round.

Rather than use the Feather Filter to create a soft border, the Eraser Tool can be used to give the image a soft irregular edge.

virtual tips

creating the video icons

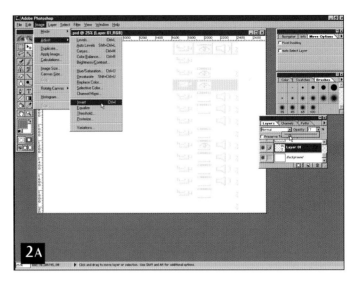

2A. Screen shots of video icons were imported into Adobe Photoshop. Using [⌘Command+T] to activate the Transform Tool, the image was enlarged in proportion by dragging the corner window handle. It was then inverted using **Image›Adjust›Invert**.

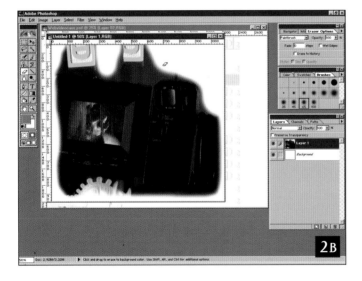

2B. A video camera and toys were scanned on the flatbed. They were then opened in Adobe Photoshop. Using the Eraser Tool, the perimeter edges were softened.

final image

2C. The video camera, toys and video icons were merged on one layer. Using **Image›Adjust›Invert**, the images were inverted to a negative.

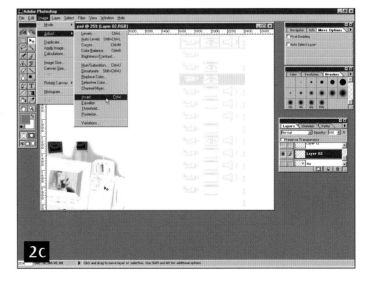

VirtualMedia A Step-By-Step Techniques Guide

creating the circles

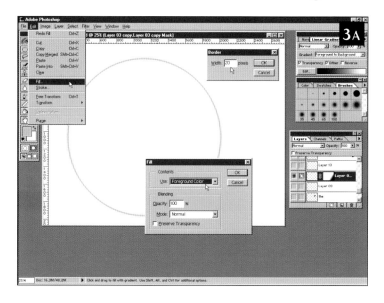

3A. A circle was made with the circular Marquee Tool. A border of 20 pixels was applied. **Edit›Fill** was opened and a yellow foreground color was applied.

3B. A mask was created using **Layer›Add Layer Mask›Reveal All**. The Gradient Tool was used to soften the edges of the circle.

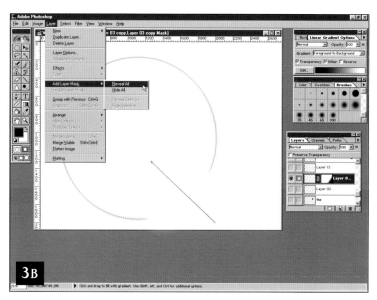

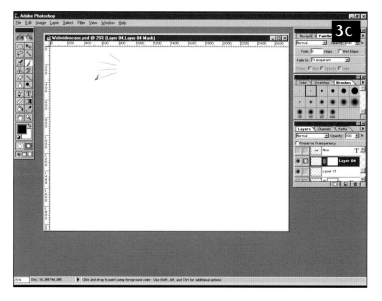

3C. Using the Paintbrush Tool, additional lines were painted. In the Paintbrush Options Fade To: Transparent was selected.

creating the typography

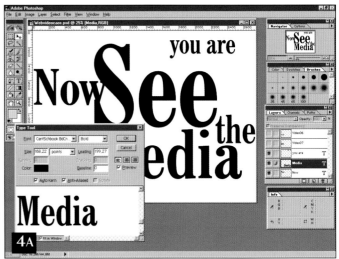

4A. Using the Type Tool, the dialog box was opened. Century Schoolbook Condensed Bold was chosen. Selections of text were typed in various point sizes and saved on different layers. The Marquee Tool selected part of the text, and [⌘Command+T] activated the Transform Tool to rotate the text.

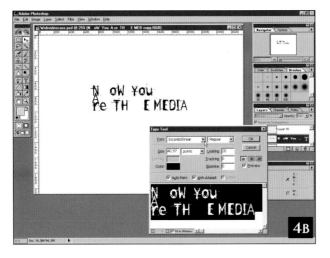

4B. Using the Type Tool, additional text was typed using the EscaildoStreak font.

final image

4C. In Pixar Typestry, "Media" was typed using Englische Demi Bold. To create the bevel, Extrude was selected with a dome bevel of 87%.

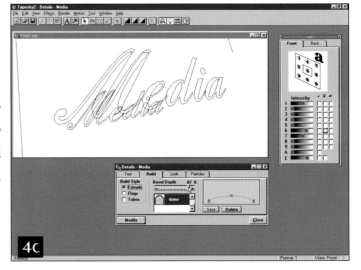

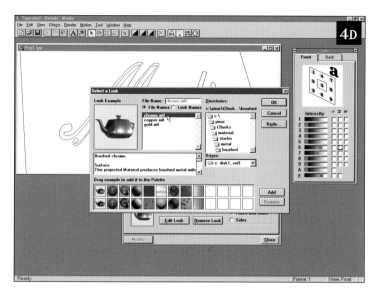

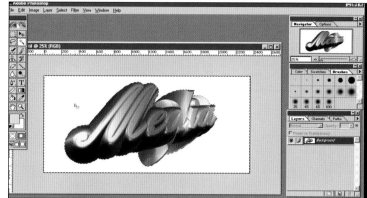

4D. In the Select A Look dialog box, the Chrome finish was selected. To produce a direct beam of light, Spot was selected as the light source in the Select A Light dialog box. The text was then selected with the Magic Wand Tool and **Select›Invert** was applied.

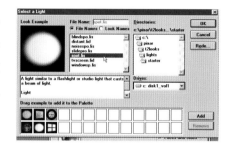

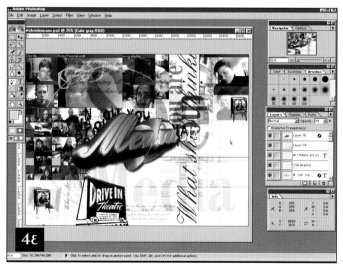

4Ɛ. All the elements were then assembled to finalize the image.

final image

INTERATIVIDADE

PURPOSE promotion

DIGITAL CREATIVE rafael peixoto ferreira, vagner monteiro

CLIENT unicamp

SOFTWARE 3D studiomax, adobe photoshop

VirtualMedia

MUNDO

PURPOSE HBO website

DIGITAL CREATIVE rafael ferreira

CLIENT time-warner/HBO brazil

SOFTWARE adobe photoshop & coreldraw

Think about the Web.
Stay in the Car and dream about your e-mails
you messages forum and virtual lovers
there is a world of there

WEB CHAOS

PURPOSE promotion
DIGITAL CREATIVE rafael ferreira
CLIENT rafa ferreira design
SOFTWARE adobe photoshop & pixar typestry

DEMO SOFTWARE DOWNLOAD WEBSITE DIRECTORY

These website addresses will give you the opportunity to download various software programs. A few of the commands in the demo tryout software have been disabled such as Save, Past and Print, but follow along with the book and experiment with the software features.

ADOBE PHOTOSHOP
http://www.adobe.com/newsfeatures/tryadobe/main.html

ADOBE ILLUSTRATOR
http://www.adobe.com/newsfeatures/tryadobe/main.html

ADOBE DIMENSIONS
http://www.adobe.com/newsfeatures/tryadobe/main.html

CHEAP VIDEO TRICK (ANDREWS FILTERS COLLECTIONS & FILTER FACTORY GALLERIES)
http://www.netins.net/showcase/wolf359/plugins.htm

EXPRESSION TOOLS SHADE
http://www.ex-tools.co.jp/index_e.htm/

MAC FILTERS (FILTER FACTORY FILTERS FOR MACINTOSH)
http://www.freefilters.com

PAINTER
http://www.metacreations.com/downloads/

RAY DREAM DESIGNER
http://www.raydream.com/downloads

DIMENSIONAL ILLUSTRATORS, INC.

VirtualMedia was produced by Dimensional Illustrators, Inc., a Philadelphia-based graphic arts publisher, to promote, honor and acknowledge excellence in the digital design industry. This premiere publication showcases the virtual how-to of creative imagery in the electronic genre of the 21st century. Dimensional Illustrators, Inc. also produces the 3Dimensional Illustrators Awards Show established in 1989 as an international competition to recognize excellence in 3Dimensional illustration. This unique exhibition honors digital and dimensional illustration, electronic artists, dimensional illustrators, modelmakers, and visual creatives and art directors.

Annual 3Dimensional Illustrators Awards Show

Unlock your best work in art direction and creation of dimensional and digital illustration. Dimension as an illustrative genre demonstrates the powerful possibilities available to all visual creatives. Take this opportunity to reveal your 3D acumen in the one show dedicated to excellence in traditional and digital contemporary dimensional illustration.

Awards

This international show presents Best of Show, Gold, Silver and Bronze awards to 3D illustrators and art directors worldwide. **Best of Show Award $1,000.**

Deadline

Entries are accepted year round. Annual Deadline June 30.

For a Call for Entries poster contact:

Nick Greco / Awards Show Coordinator
Dimensional Illustrators, Inc.
362 Second Street Pike / Suite 112
Southampton, Pennsylvania 18966 USA
215.953.1415 **Telephone**
215.953.1697 **Fax**
http://www.3DimIllus.com **Website**
dimension@3DimIllus.com **Email**

Artists Directory

MARGARET CARSELLO
Carsello Creative
P.O. Box G
Hinsdale, IL 60522
Phone: 630.794.9120
Fax: 630.794.9131
Email: mcarsello@mediaone.net

JENSON DESIGNAHOLIX
34742 Sunset Drive
Oconomowoc, WI 53066
Phone: 414.646.5095
Fax: 414.646.5095

RAFAEL PEIXOTO FERREIRA
Rafa Ferreira Design
Av. Orosimbo Maia, 2090 a17
Campinas, SP 13024-030 Brazil
Phone: 55 019 254-3360
Email: rfdesign@dglnet.com.br
Website: http://www.rafael.ferreira.nom.br

LISA JOHNSTON
digitalari
2008 Rutger Street
St. Louis, MI 63104
Phone: 314.283.4500
Email: lisa@digitalari.com
Website: http://www.digitalari.com

TONY KLASSEN
1429 Furnleigh Lane
Chesterton, IN 46304
Phone: 219.926.2045
Fax: 219.926.7648
Email: klassen@netnitco.net
Website: http://www.phantaz.com

SUSAN LEVAN
LeVan/Barbee Studio
30 Ipswich Street / #211
Boston, MA 02215
Phone: 617.536.6828
Fax: 617.421.0907
Email: slveb@world.std.com

GUSTAVO MACHADO
Anti-Materia Design
Rua Itu, 234 / 92 - CEP 13.025-340
Campinas, Brazil
Phone: 55-19-255-6829
Fax: 55-19-255-6829
Email: gmachado_design@hotmail.com
Website: http://www.peoplecomputacao.com.br/webdesigner/gustavomachado

SCOTT PETTY
Beehive Design
11991 Driftstone Drive
Fishers, IN 46038
Phone: 317-842-2412
Fax: 317-842-2412
Email: spetty@iei.net

CHET PHILLIPS
Chet Phillips Illustration
6527 Del Norte
Dallas, TX 75225-2620
Phone: 214.987.4344
Fax: 214.987.2234
Email: chet@airmail.net
Website: http://web2.airmail.net/chet

JASON HOWARD STATTS
Post Office Box 16626
Savannah, GA 31416
Email: thinearth@worldnet.att.net

Rep: Three In A Box, Inc.
Phone: 416.367.2446 Toronto, Canada
Website: http://www.threeinabox.com

YASUTAKA TAGA
925 Hiyodorijima
Toyama-Shi,
Toyama-Ken 930-0885 Japan
Phone: 81.764.31.6735
Fax: 81.764.33.9265
Email: taga@po2.nsknet.or.jp

TOM WHITE
Tom White Images
750 Columbus Avenue / #2E
New York, NY 10025
Phone: 212.866.7841
Fax: 212.866.8166
Email: tom@twimages.com

New Digital Graphic Books
From Dimensional Illustrators, Inc.

ExtremeGraphics

Edited by: Kathleen Ziegler and Nick Greco

Digital creatives reach far beyond the limits of cyberspace in this premiere publication of *ExtremeGraphics*, a benchmark collection of electronic imagery. Experience the infinite capabilities of the computer as more than 300 full-color images break graphic rules and shatter your concept of reality. More than 30 digital visionaries featured in *ExtremeGraphics* exemplify the limitless possibilities of the new-media generation. Each provocative image transforms reality and illusion into a shifting, quixotic vision never before imagined. Journey beyond the limits of the known visual universe. *ExtremeGraphics* will propel you through the creative cosmos of cyberspace, exceed the limits of your expectations and push them to the extreme.
Cover Image: Michael Morgenstern

DigitalFocus *The New Media of Photography*

Edited by: Kathleen Ziegler and Nick Greco

Experience the powerful imagery of digital photography. *DigitalFocus* explores the essence of both the explosive and impressive fusion of photography and digital illustration. This premiere edition applauds the diversity of this photographic genre and alters forever our perception of the camera and the computer. With more than 300 full-color examples, *DigitalFocus* discusses inventive software techniques, exposing the interrelationships that exist between the origin of the idea, the creative process, and the final image. This is a vital publication for all creative visionaries seeking to explore the cyber-technology of new media photography. Chapters include: Advertising, Business, Sports, Surreal, People, Editorial and Media. *Cover Image: Nick Koudis*

Digitalink *digital design and advertising*

Edited by: Kathleen Ziegler and Nick Greco

Take a quantum leap into the electrifying age of digital design and advertising. Immerse yourself in the cutting-edge genius of computer-generated imagery. Witness the fresh, raw enthusiasm of the digital illustrator. In this showcase edition of *Digitalink*, you will find more than 300 captivating digital illustrations in which the ingenuity of electronic art and advertising collide. Each provocative chapter explodes with details on the software, methods and techniques that shift electronic design into high gear. This book will both inspire and excite you as you delve into the limitless potential of this new-wave media. Chapters include: Magazine and Editorial Advertising, Direct Mail, Posters, Annual Reports, Book Covers and Brochures.

VirtualMedia

A Digital Step-By-Step Techniques Guide

Edited by: Kathleen Ziegler and Nick Greco

In **VirtualMedia A Digital Step-by-Step Techniques Guide**, digital aficionados reveal their approaches through twelve step-by-step projects. The five chapters — Digital Collage, 3D Modeling, CyberIllustration, Filters and Effects and Typography — share a cross-section of a unique range of techniques through a variety of software, including Adobe Photoshop, MetaCreations Fractal Painter, Adobe Dimensions, Expression Tools' Shade, RayDream Designer and Adobe Illustrator. Virtual tips from each artist offer software shortcuts and insights for the digital designer. As each step-by-step project unfolds, follow along as the final image develops on the page. Then, use the book's directory of website addresses to download demonstration software featured in this book.

Cover Images: Tony Klassen, (Cover Insets: Susan LeVan, Jason Statts, Tom White)

CyberPalette

A Digital Step-By-Step Guide

Edited by: Kathleen Ziegler and Nick Greco

CyberPalette A Digital Step-By-Step Guide features the artistry of ten leading electronic design creatives. Each digital illustrator presents a methodical sequence of steps designed to divulge each facet of his or her creative process, layer by layer, from conceptual idea to final output image. Discover the techniques and software these artists use to achieve their astounding art. **CyberPalette** is an exceptional electronic pictorial presentation designed to stimulate your creative digital energies. Experience the infinite possibilities of the new-age technology and enter the fascinating realm of computer-generated artistry: Let your imagination soar through cyberspace. *Cover Image: Ben Tomita, (Cover Inset: Pamela Hobbs)*

More Paper Sculpture

A Step-By-Step Guide

Edited by: Kathleen Ziegler and Nick Greco

Expand your creative capabilities and experience a fascinating journey through the enchanting realm of paper sculpture. Ten internationally distinguished artists present all-new, hand selected projects and gallery pieces culled from their personal portfolios. This full-color, step-by-step guide features more than 300 photographs, from layout to finished sculpture. **More Paper Sculpture** is a valuable resource for the novice or professional seeking a delightful medium for artistic expression. Stimulate your creative energies and expand your marketability in the illustration and fine art industries. This absorbing and inspirational edition reveals the technical skills used by professional paper sculptors for enjoyment, as well as, for profit.

Cover Image: Carol Jeanotilla

Quantity	-	Title	Price	-	Int'l Shipping Add $5.00	-	PA Residents Add 7%	-	TOTAL
	-	**VirtualMedia**	**$34.95** *(includes shipping within USA)*						
	-	**CyberPalette**	**$32.95** *(includes shipping within USA)*						
	-	**More Paper Sculpture**	**$32.95** *(includes shipping within USA)*						

Shipping Address: (Please Print Clearly)

Name_____

Firm_____

Address_____

City_____ State_____ Zip_____ (Country)_____

_____Check (drawn on a U.S. bank only) _____Visa/MasterCard _____MoneyOrder

Credit Card#_____

Signature_____ Exp. Date_____

Phone_____

Send Payment to:

Dimensional Illustrators, Inc.
362 2nd Street Pike/Suite 112
Southampton, PA 18966 USA

215-953-1415 Phone
215-953-1697 Fax (24 hours)
dimension@3dimillus.com **Email**
http://www.3dimillus.com **Online Orders**

U.S. Orders Shipped in 2 weeks.
Overseas orders shipped in 4-6 weeks.